Introducing
the

Family Limited
Partnership.

Second Edition

How to Save Megabucks In Taxes
and
Maintain Control of Your Assets.

Charles S. Stoll CPA, CFP, CEP, PFS
and
Ronald C. White, Esq.

Written with
Joyce K. Reynolds

This publication is designed to provide accurate and authoritative information in regard to the subject matter covered. It is sold with the understanding that the publisher is not engaged in rendering legal, accounting, or other professional service. While legal, tax, and accounting issues have been checked with sources believed to be reliable, some material may be affected by changes in the laws or in the interpretations of such laws since the man-uscript for this book was completed. For that reason the accuracy and completeness of such information and the opinions based there on are not guaranteed. In addition, state and local tax laws or procedural rules may have a material impact on the general recommendations made by the authors, and the strategies outlined in this book may not be suitable for every individual. If legal, accounting, tax, investment, or other expert advice is required, obtain the services of a competent practitioner.

Library of Congress Catalog Card Number: 98-074585

ISBN: 0-9654605-1-7

Fortune Press Publishers, Inc.
129 NW 13th Street, Suite D-26
Boca Raton, FL 33432
1-800-950-9116

This book is dedicated to the one of world's greatest men and a true genius with money, Bob Castiglione.

We also dedicate this book to our wives - Fabienne Stoll and Shelley White - for all their support during the countless hours spent away from home in seminars and in book compilation and writing sessions.

Table of Contents

Introduction

Chapter 1

The Billionaire's Tale.
The incredible story of how Sam Walton, founder of Wal-Mart, used a Family Partnership to maintain control of his business empire and save billions in taxes.

Chapter 2

The Doctor Knows Best.
Read how one successful physician used a Family Limited Partnership to save estate tax and keep control of his assets through family and intra-family loans and valuation discounts.

Chapter 3

Protecting the Wealth in Citizen/Resident Alien Marriages.
This discussion covers many of the fine points of change in the laws governing deductions, estate tax and trust alternatives - including Qualified Domestic Trust (QDOT) - for the citizen/resident alien married couple.

Chapter 4

Advance Financial Planning for Middle America.
Understand how Uniform Transfers to Minors' accounts can assist in good planning for underage children and become aware of rules regarding securities portfolios and how the Family Partnership can be of assistance in cases of divorce.

Chapter 5

The Guide to Life Insurance Ownership.
Learn how to advantageously use this frequently misunderstood, misused and under-utilized but important financial tool.

Chapter 6

Financial Focus for Doctors, Professionals and Business Owners.

Saving taxes is only one of the many concerns facing professionals and business owners. Here's help in keeping your business or practice out of potential harm from creditors, the IRS, even extended family members.

Chapter 7

Getting the Best of Medicaid and Other Suggestions for the Aged.

This invaluable chapter includes information on the sensitive and serious matter of Medicaid planning along with a discussion about financial options which can help the aged gift away assets but also keep control of them too.

Chapter 8

Divorce and Family Financial Affairs.

Today's responsibly-constructed financial plans must take into account potential financial upsets and solutions surrounding the issue of divorce.

Chapter 9

Being Elderly Doesn't Mean Being Out of Control.
You've earned it and made it grow. So whether you're 60 or 90, protect your money through proper estate planning; thus eliminating any fear of being rendered old and poor.

Chapter 10

A State in Point: Florida's Intangible Tax.
Use this example as a benchmark for understanding how people with large portfolios can legally avoid paying intangible tax.

Chapter 11

Monetary Miscellany.
Get the details on some powerful options for Family Limited Partnerships including: gifting and valuation discounts; multi-layered partnerships; offshore and irrevocable trusts.

Chapter 12

The Promise of the Family Limited Partnership.
Use this handy, detailed section to determine just how
much you can expect to save using a Family Limited
Partnership.

Chapter 13

Questions and Answers
Designed as a quick-reference guide, this chapter will
answer many questions and lead you to more in-depth
information on others.

APPENDIX

1. **Investment Company Rules**
2. **A checklist for Estate and Financial Planning**
3. **Index of Professionals**

Preface

In the years that have passed since we put together our first Family Limited Partnership, we have learned a great deal about how this powerful tool can assist in enhancing and maintaining intra-family values and relationships.

We have, in fact, successfully used Family Limited Partnerships to meet so many challenging situations that we felt compelled to gather up our various experiences and ideas into one complete handbook for the benefit of a broader audience. We did so in order to assist people in developing a basic understanding of the Family Limited Partnership and how this vehicle can be used to intelligently and sensitively direct and protect a family's assets.

Additionally, we wanted to highlight the primary and motivating force behind the use of the Family Limited Partnership. Overwhelmingly, we have observed that these Partnerships are preferred by those who wish to make an expression of love for family, one which underscores a desire for their loved ones to get - and keep - as much as possible of the fruits of their life's work.

Helen Walton, widow of Wal-Mart's Sam Walton, probably said it best when discussing their own Family Limited Partnership:

"It was great money-wise, but there was another aspect to it; the relationship that was established among the children and with the family. It developed their sense of responsibility toward one another. You just can't beat that."

Introduction

We have designed this book to allow you to learn how Family Limited Partnerships can help you solve the problems and avoid many of the costs that usually become attached to wealth you have accumulated or inherited. It is also intended to serve as a primer for attorneys and accountants who want to learn more about this exciting topic.

At the onset, we'd like to make it clear that this book is not just for the wealthy or the very wealthy. Quite to the contrary, you will see, in scanning the Table of Contents, that we have included numerous, easily understandable examples of the myriad of benefits of Family Limited Partnerships to a wide range of family and business situations. The intention is to give you a working understanding of what it takes to set up a Family Limited Partnership and what you might expect to get out of the process. Additionally, we have included a Question/Answer section which is a quick reference to chapters containing further information regarding your specific areas of interest.

People choose to use Family Limited Partnerships for various reasons and, despite the implications of the name, these agreements are limited only by the creativity and imagination of the clients and their advisors. This, in conjunction with the fact of the complex nature of the Family Limited Partnership, necessitates our noting the fact that this book is in no way intended to replace competent counsel.

We, therefore, strongly urge you to consult your personal attorney, accountant or financial advisor and seek guidance in the proper design of your Family Limited Partnership. To assist you towards implementation, we have included in the back of this book, a list of professionals who have expressed a familiarity with and interest in this topic and hope you will consider using them as advisors in preparation of your Family Partnership.

Finally, whatever financial goal you seek to accomplish, we hope you will find the following material useful in helping you keep control of all of your valued assets. Please feel free to visit our World Wide Web page for further information.

Charles S. Stoll and Ronald C. White

Home Page address: http://www.stoll-fin.com

Acknowledgements

This book would not be complete without giving our thanks to following people:

Mindy King, our marketing director for her dedication in managing this project from beginning to end.

Doretha Walker-Faircloth, Executive Administrative Manager for Stoll Financial Corp. for all her long hours, devotion and her amazing talent for getting things done.

Lynn Keating, Administrative Assistant for Stoll Financial Corp., for all her time and patience.

Barbara Carter-Hanson, Legal Secretary to Ronald White for all her time and patience.

Special thanks to our sons, Preston and Alex Stoll and Johnathan and Christopher White for their patience and understanding of all the extra hours at the office.

Finally, no acknowlegement would be complete without thanking our clients, whose experiences became the basis of this book.

CHAPTER
1

The Billionaire's Tale.

As founder and CEO of Wal-Mart, the one-time largest family-held corporation in America, Sam Walton was faced with the incredible financial challenge of keeping his enormous empire together not only for himself but for the benefit of his entire family.

While few of us will ever be asked to deal with monetary issues of quite this magnitude, we can, nonetheless, learn from the brilliant strategies that Sam Walton put to use as he uncovered the power and flexibility of the Family Partnership to achieve the end of retaining control of his finances and protecting all of his assets.

Let's take a look at what attracted Sam to the Family Partnership and how he managed - after becoming the richest man in America in just 40 years - to leave an incredible 80% of his wealth to his family estate tax-free, without ever loosing control of his assets. Then, we'll see how we can apply what he learned to other, perhaps less sizable but equally important, situations to the same positive end.

How It All Began.

Sam Walton was not born of wealth. This fact may surprise those who assume, in order to amass the kind of enormous assets he eventually accumulated, that he must have started out with a considerable estate. Actually, the key to Sam Walton's wealth was held by his father-in-law, L.S. Robson, who was a very wealthy Arkansas businessman in the 1950's. And, for those who are once again tempted to jump to the conclusion that great inherited wealth accounted for Sam Walton's success, we'll tell you right now - that was not the case.

In reading Walton's autobiography along with the innumerable articles written about the entire Walton family, another more fascinating and complete picture of how this empire was built comes to light. In these various writings, we find that, rather than actually benefiting from the Robson fortune via his wife, Helen, Sam Walton uncovered an even greater asset in understanding how his father-in-law had made excellent use of at least one Family Partnership in his own estate plan. This judicious instrument ultimately provided the basis for Walton's incredible financial story beginning early in his business career when Sam Walton began experiencing the challenge of what we today know as income taxes.

In the 1940's and 50's, when Walton's Ben Franklin retail store was beginning to thrive, taxes could go up to 94% and, with the success of his stores, that's just about where Sam landed. With Sam handing over those kinds of percentages to the IRS, it was clear that, unless he could make some changes, he was not going to be able to internally generate the capital which would allow him to expand and grow his retail operation.

In discussing this dilemma with his wife, Helen, she suggested to Sam that he talk with her father, the pivotal Mr. Robson, about how he was successfully managing a similar situation. Thus it was that Sam Walton found and understood the enormous benefits of the Family Partnership. In taking up this topic with Sam, Mr. Robson explained how he had been using a Family Partnership to protect his earnings by gifting interest of this Partnership to his children, taking advantage of the fact that, in those days, there was no "kiddy" tax. Immediately, Sam saw the possibilities for his situation.

With each of his children in an individual tax bracket amounting to as little as 3%, Walton quickly understood that for every dollar of income that he and Helen transferred to them, they would escape from a 94% tax bracket instead paying as little as 3%. This income transfer alone amounted to a potential savings to the family of up to 91 cents on every dollar. As the story goes, it was just this 91-cents-per-dollar savings that was reinvested to create the beginnings of the Wal-Mart empire.

While old records of this business are not public making accurate calculations a bit difficult, it is interesting to imagine what those early investment dollars would equal today in Wal-Mart stock. We believe it's entirely reasonable to assume that a sizable amount of the current wealth of the Walton family is due to the early income tax savings that were achieved through the Family Partnership agreements that Sam Walton set into motion on the advice of his father-in-law. We might also add that all this was accomplished without giving up control of the store.

The Walton Plan.

Through the strategic use of the Family Partnership and the accompanying world-renowned success of Wal-Mart,

Sam and Helen Walton have supplied the perfect model for understanding how this powerful vehicle can work in numerous other situations. Using available records of their agreements, we can study the blueprint which was drawn up by this family.

Sam Walton had two primary goals with regard to his growing empire. He wanted to maintain absolute control of his business, and protect his money and assets. Initially, in a formal written document, the Waltons set up a Family Partnership agreement which spelled out in clear detail just how business was to be done, who was to control it and who would determine the amounts and distribution of profits that would be payable to the Partners, the family members.

Sam and Helen then transferred into the Partnership their ownership of the stores which, eventually, became the Wal-Mart chain. Next and most important, Sam and Helen gave their children "part-ownership" of the Partnership, meaning that the Partnership owned the business and the children owned a portion of the Partnership. Thus, in keeping with Sam Walton's desires, this private document or Partnership agreement was, in actuality, the controlling instrument for the business and the paper which allowed each Walton child to own something without having any control over it.

Income Tax Ramifications.

One of the most significant and highly attractive aspects of the Family Partnership is found in the tax ramifications of such an agreement. Simply and boldly put, a Partnership does not pay any income tax. Rather, it calculates and reports income based on each Partner's interest in the Partnership. Let's see through the following example just how this works.

Suppose that Mom and Dad have a $100,000 Treasury Bond which is paying 8% in yearly interest. Without an agreement, each year they would receive and have to pay tax in their 39.6% income tax bracket on the earned interest of $8,000, 8% of $100,000. Therefore, their investment is costing them approximately $3,168 annually in federal income tax.

Let's look at what would happen if, instead, Mom and Dad transferred their $100,000 bond into a Partnership and, over time, gifted 80% of the Partnership to their children. Assuming that their children are in a lower tax bracket - a 15% tax bracket, for example - a tax savings such as the following could result:

Under such an agreement, the children own 80% of the Partnership and, thus, report and pay federal income tax in their bracket on their 80% share of the interest in the Partnership. In other terms, instead of paying the $3,168 that their parents have owed annually, the children are now going to pay approximately $960 which is calculated by taking their tax bracket of 15% times the $8,000 interest times their 80% ownership.

Meanwhile, the parents own 20% of the bond represented by their 20% ownership of the Partnership and have only to pay income tax on that 20%. In their 39.6% tax bracket, this amounts to approximately $634 which, added to the $960 the children now pay, totals $1,594 in federal income tax as opposed to the $3,168 which was annually due without the Family Partnership agreement. This represents an annual savings of $1,574 which can be used or invested for the benefit of everyone involved.

Just like the Waltons who wanted to save on income tax while keeping control of their business, this family can accomplish the same goals for themselves and their investments by setting up a Family Partnership and having it hold their treasury bond.

Transferring Appreciating Property to Family Partnerships Saves Taxes.

Over the years, Sam and Helen Walton continued to give part ownership of their Family Partnership to their children each time transferring a bit of income tax liability to a lower bracket, hence, saving more money while building the family's multi-billion-dollar empire. In like fashion, the Family Partnership can be used to ensure continued and additional tax savings to those who wish to maintain control of their assets while benefiting their families. This is especially good news for those who anticipate having to pay hefty estate tax.

Businesses and securities portfolios appreciate in a variety of ways. Some grow because of increased earnings, some simply grow at interest. But, the underlying assets - real estate, copyrights, patents, oil and gas properties represented by these portfolios appreciate, usually increasing in value over time. The Family Partnership can be used to move any appreciation out of an estate for the purpose of saving taxes and keeping control of any such assets.

Sam and Helen Walton accomplished it this way. In order to save income taxes, they set up a Partnership and transferred ownership interests to their family members. While we don't know the exact amount due to the privacy of the agreement, we think it's safe to say the Waltons saved a fortune in income tax, saving an additional fortune in estate tax because the appreciation on the business was transferred to the children's estates. And, as they owned a percentage of the Partnership, they also owned a percentage of the appreciation of the property the Partnership owned. In this manner, as the value of Walton Family Enterprises grew, the children got rich right along with - and maybe even faster than - Sam and Helen.

In fact, it has been reported that on his death Sam owned only 10% of Walton Family Enterprises, the Partnership. Helen reportedly owned another 10% and the rest of the family owned 80%. If, for example, the family was worth $25 billion, Sam owned only $2.5 billion yet the Partnership agreement enabled him to control the full $25 billion in Wal-Mart stock while retaining complete authority over the corporation he so brilliantly built.

Sam and Helen Walton Said It Best.

At the time of publication of his autobiography, *Sam Walton, Made in America: My Story,* Sam said regarding their Family agreement,

"The Partnership works in a number of different ways. First, it enables us to control Wal-Mart through the family and keep it together, rather than having it sold off in pieces, haphazardly. We still own 38 percent of the company's stock today, which is an unusually large stake for anyone to hold in an outfit the size of Wal-Mart, and that's the best protection there is against the takeover raiders.

It's something that any family who has faith in its strength as a unit and in the growth potential of its business can do. The transfer of ownership was made so long ago that we didn't have to pay substantial gift or inheritance taxes on it. The principle behind this is simple: the best way to reduce paying estate taxes is to give your assets away before they appreciate.

It turned out to be a great philosophy and a great strategy and I certainly wouldn't have figured it out way back then without the advice of Helen's father. It wasn't lavish or exorbitant and that was part of the plan - to keep the family together as well as maintain a sense of balance in our standards."

Through the setting up of this Family Partnership, Sam Walton saved approximately $12.5 billion in estate tax representing approximately one-half the net worth of his family which would otherwise have been owed to the IRS. As a result, those direct and mutual fund shareholders of Wal-Mart outside his gifted family circle can also thank Sam Walton from keeping, to the benefit of their portfolios, that $12.5 billion worth of stock from having to come to market in order to pay those taxes. As was his way, Sam Walton acted not only out of largesse to his family but to his shareholders as well.

Helen Walton, too, became an advocate of the Family Partnership, in fact, pinpointing the most appreciative aspect of this financial vehicle. "It was great money wise, but there was another aspect to it; the relationship that was established among the children and with the family. It developed their sense of responsibility toward one another. You just can't beat that."

In Summary.

Sam and Helen Walton embarked upon an estate and financial plan based on a concept offered to them by Helen's father, L. S. Robson, a very successful Arkansas businessman. As a result, they transferred their business interests into a Partnership and then transferred interests in that Partnership to their children. In the end and while largely undocumented, we can assume that the Partnership accomplished considerable income tax savings which assisted Sam in creating his great fortune.

Additionally, the strategy paid off with estate tax savings in the billions that was brought about by the transfer of appreciation out of Sam's estate by way of the Partnership. More importantly, the strategy of using a Family Partnership kept Sam in charge of his companies and, to a large degree, his family's finances.

A lot more particulars of this story are captured in Sam's autobiography, *Sam Walton, Made in America: My Story*. It's fascinating reading including the suggested irony that Sam Walton's early high income tax bracket was probably due, in part, to the income that was generated from his wife's ownership of interest in the Robson Partnership, the very same that was the inspiration for Sam Walton's success. If so, it would seem a worthwhile price to have paid for his acquaintance with the powerful, flexible and protective Family Partnership.

This story about one of America's richest families telling us in their own words what their Family Partnership did for them and how it contributed to their success as business people and as a family means alot. In the long run, they also gave us a fine blueprint to follow in achieving similar savings for untold others.

CHAPTER
2

The Doctor Knows Best.

One of the countless others who would eventually benefit from the intelligent, flexible features of the Family Partnership arrived quietly at one of our evening seminars. This quite distinguished gentleman sat interestedly through our presentation on Partnerships, then slipped out before we could arrange any introductions. Weeks later during an appointment that he had requested, we discovered that our guest and soon to be new client was a renowned neurosurgeon who had earned and saved considerable sums of money through his successful practice and wise investments. And, our doctor was in pursuit of a plan that would provide the best financial protection for himself, his wife and his eight children.

He stated that he was looking for a plan that would keep his sizable estate - which was well into the millions - intact and firmly in his control. He told us that he had attended dozens of estate planning meetings offered by stockbrokers, attorneys and insurance agents but he had not heard of a plan that would suitably meet his needs until he attended our seminar on Family Partnerships.

His previous disinterest in estate planning was primarily due to the fact that most such plans seemed to hinge on the doctor handing over his millions to his children, a concept which held no appeal for this financially astute physician for a number of good reasons. First, he simply did not wish to relinquish control over his investments and assets by gifting them away as had been suggested through normal estate planning. The doctor already knew that he could annually give $10,000 to each of his family members but that would mean writing checks or transferring securities of $80,000 per year. In fact, if he included his in-laws and grandchildren, the annual gifting figure could easily go over $400,000, not a plan which made our doctor happy. So, he continued his search for a way to reduce his estate tax without this type of yearly arrangement.

Moreover and of even greater concern to the doctor was the fact that, if he wrote those kinds of checks each year, he would be relinquishing control over his money. Yes, his children would be in receipt of the funds but years of experience had taught him that he was a better money manager than any of his eight children. The doctor knew if he followed this plan, his valued estate would be at risk. Additionally, his aim was not to simply contribute regular cash gifts to the children which would likely result in nothing more than enhancing their lifestyle. In short, he did not want to give away his assets at the risk of their being ill-used or wastefully spent. Therefore, the conventional estate plans which were based on making those kinds of gifts simply did not appeal to him.

We had, however, keenly interested him in the subject of Family Partnerships at our seminar. In thinking over all he had heard that evening, the doctor realized that a Family Partnership could accomplish all of his goals while resolving his previously mentioned concerns. We, therefore, immediately set up a Family Partnership and transferred into it a small brokerage account. From that point on, our client has continued to annually transfer to each of his children the allowed sum of $10,000, but now, instead of cash, it is given as an interest in the Partnership. So, rather than costing the doctor dollars, each $10,000 gift of Partnership interest under this arrangement has saved him $5,000 in estate tax. Additionally, whatever growth that takes place in the children's Partnership shares is also kept out of the doctor's estate thus saving him additional taxes. The Partnership was also designed to prevent the children from selling or borrowing money against their Partnership interests. The doctor, therefore, not only reduced his estate tax by a wide margin but got to keep his money safe as well.

When we look at the details of this plan - examining first any costs to the doctor - we see that, aside from some minor maintenance fees, the doctor incurred no estate planning expenses. He simply transferred to his children part ownership of the Limited Partnership without even having to write a check and, certainly, without giving up any control of his investments.

Further, we see that another of the doctor's objectives was easily and inoffensively met through the Partnership. As the children received only part interest in the Partnership, the equity transferred to his children was not subject to waste, misuse or loss through divorce, bad business decisions or simply poor investing practices. The invested moneys stayed, by stipulation, right where they started, safely in a brokerage account. The doctor, meanwhile, kept control of his funds and continued investing just as he had over prior years. Through the Family Partnership, the doctor had clearly accomplished all that he had desired to achieve of his financial plan.

Next, the doctor revealed an even more creative strategy for keeping his Family Partnership in good stead. It turned out that while he had not made all those cash gifts that conventional estate planning people kept urging him to make, the doctor had been equally generous with his children in other ways such as allowing them loans and advances for new cars, homes, even new businesses. When any such loans were made, the doctor did require the children to sign notes bearing interest with payment stipulations. The intention here was that upon his death these moneys would be accounted for in his estate with each of his children being handled equitably.

However well-intended these plans were, difficulties arose when, on occasion, his children failed to make their loan payments. In fact, when the doctor once heard himself referred to as the "International Bank of Dad" by one of his children, he knew he had a problem that finally needed to be addressed. Rather than continuing to find himself in the uncomfortable spot of either enforcing the notes and suing his children or just doing nothing, the doctor came up with a brilliant solution.

Using the Family Partnership for the solution, he contributed all loans and notes into the Partnership in exchange for Partnership interests which he could transfer to his children. After making these arrangements, the doctor convened a meeting of his children and explained the ramifications of this transaction as it applied to any outstanding loans.

"As of this day," the doctor told his children, "I have contributed all the notes that are owed to me into the Family

Partnership. This assures me that everything in my estate will be handled fairly and equitably between all of you. From this point forward none of you owes me a dime - not even for any notes you have taken out. All those moneys are now owed to the Partnership and, therefore, to your brothers and sisters. In fact, as of this day, I have waived any interest that is past due, but, remember, the Partnership must make money so you must realize that every outstanding loan is now accruing interest. Additionally, if any of you need to borrow money in the future, rather than borrowing it from me, you must borrow it from the Partnership. Now, are there any questions?"

The doctor was met with total silence.

He continued, "If, as you have on occasion in the past, you find yourselves having to be late with your loan payments, you won't be coming to me but rather to one of your sisters, either Jean or Joyce (two of his most frugal children), who I've asked to represent the Partnership in these matters. In other words, if you must be tardy or skip a payment, you'll need to get their permission."

Now you can see what we meant when we said the doctor knows best. Providing us with an invaluable new suggestion on how to handle intra-family Partnership loans, the doctor managed to involve all of his family members in the responsible management of the agreement, making it all but impossible for his children to delay or avoid the repayment of their debts. He not only established the basis for excellent financial communication between those that he loved, but also managed to bring his estate back into equilibrium. In short and in a very creative manner, the doctor accomplished all that he had set out to do and much more.

In Summary.

Our client, the brilliant neurosurgeon and financial investor, certainly proved to us how financially savvy he was when he chose a Family Partnership. Through this agreement, he was able to reduce his taxable estate by making gifts of large sums of money to his family members without subjecting the funds to risks of misuse or consumption. Further, he wisely used the Partnership to restore some discipline to certain family members regarding their loan repayment practices. As a result, the doctor now has an ever-decreasing estate tax bill with more control over his investments.

Advanced Planning Pointer #1
Lifetime Unified Credit Exemption

It would further advance this client's goals if he and his wife decided to each use up their Lifetime Unified Credit Exemption. In this instance, a one-time combined transfer of $1,250,000 would speed up their estate tax savings as it transfers the $1,250,000 outside their taxable estate. This strategy carries no current cash cost and could save considerable additional estate tax as the earnings and appreciation on the $1,250,000 would also be outside the parents' taxable estate. By 2007 as the credit grows, the parents could give a total or $2,000,000 to the next generation.

Advanced Planning Pointer #2

Valuation Discounts and More Tax Savings

Also in this case, further improvement could be realized by combining the above-mentioned Lifetime Unified Credit Exemption with the use of an appraisal from a independent firm that would attest to the value of the transferred Partnership interests. (Note: We are not speaking here about an appraisal of the contents of the Partnership, but rather an appraisal of what the Partnership interests themselves are worth, which could be quite a different story.)

For example, let's suppose a man named Joe has a $1,000,000 in cash and wants to give $100,000 of it to his son, Joe, Jr. If the father makes this gift by writing a check, it is clearly worth $100,000. Then Joe, Jr. takes control of the money and can do whatever he wants to with it.

However, with this same $1,000,000 in mind, let's see what could happen if we slightly changed the situation. Let's say that instead of giving Joe, Jr. a check, his father forms a corporation and contributes the $1,000,000 to it. He then gives Joe, Jr. 10% of the new corporation's stock, which is theoretically worth $100,000 as it represents 10% of a corporation that has capital of $1,000,000. But, in this case, there are other factors that need to be considered in the appraisal of the securities transferred from Joe to Joe, Jr.

One of the primarily jobs an appraiser will have is to determine what this corporation would actually be worth to a buyer who had reasonable knowledge of all the relevant facts. The answer might be that to a potential buyer, knowing that he or she would have no control over the corporation, the election of directors or officers and might never see any of the capital until the 90% owner wanted that to happen - the value of 10% interest in the corporation could be considerably less than a $100,000. In other words, it is how assets are owned and controlled that affects their value. The lack of control and restrictions placed on a minority shareholder interest could result in an appraisal of the entire asset at a value for estate and gift tax purposes of less than the value without such restrictions.

Historically, discounts have existed in both publicly- and privately-held corporations. As a result, Barrons weekly newspaper contains a section on closed end funds which lists corporations that are trading at discounts to their net asset value. The reason for this is that, just like the above mentioned $1,000,000 corporation, the shareholders of these companies can't force the redemption of their publicly-traded shares at their net asset value. They are worth less and valued at less than what they would be if the shareholders could force redemption. Further, the discounts would probably be greater if the shares were not publicly traded.

A Family Partnership is similar to the closed end fund or privately-held corporate stock in that, using the proper statutory provisions and limitations, the children cannot force their interests to be paid out in cash. By simply contributing money or assets to a properly-structured Family Partnership, there could be a reduced value for the Gift and Estate tax man to tax. For more in-depth discussion on this topic, see Chapter 1.

CHAPTER
3

Protecting the Wealth
in Citizen/Resident
Alien Marriages.

A s our world continues to become more widely traveled, the incidence of multi-national marriages has increasingly provoked changes in U.S. laws regarding the finances of U.S. citizens married to foreign citizens. One of the major changes that was made prevents a person who has married a foreign national from transferring his or her estate to the foreign spouse who, in the past, would have been free to leave the United States with those assets without paying gift and estate taxes.

In other words, under prior circumstances and before the law changed, a non-U.S. citizen surviving spouse could have legally left the U.S. with the proceeds of the U.S. citizen's estate untaxed. This loophole has since been closed by the IRS, causing other problems for the non-U.S. citizen spouse.

In 1989, the U.S. government passed a law which put

parameters on the previously unlimited marital deduction that allowed a U.S. citizen to leave his or her wealth, in its entirety, to a foreign spouse. Under the new law, this type of unlimited bequest is only allowable if the surviving spouse is also a U.S. citizen. However, the law still provides a couple of ways to get the unlimited deduction, thus avoiding the massive estate tax at the death of the U.S. citizen spouse. Here are some provisions that help couples who fit this category deal with the new laws:

1) The non-U.S. citizen surviving spouse can become a U.S. citizen within nine months following the death of the spouse and then file an estate tax return.

2) Alternatively, the non-citizen surviving spouse can set up and fund a special trust called a Qualified Domestic Trust (QDOT) within that same 9-month time period. This would defer the estate tax on the assets until the surviving spouse's death. However, little case law has come down to define how all this would be managed should the estate plan of the decedent not specifically provide for the QDOT trust in his or her will; thus, making it all the more important for any wealthy non-U.S. citizen or one married to a wealthy U.S. citizen to have a proper and current plan.

The QDOT Trust

Here's how we can assist the U.S. citizen and his or her foreign national spouse in protecting their assets. First, in order for the estate tax to be deferred until the death of the surviving spouse, the assets must be placed in a special trust called a Qualified Domestic Trust or QDOT with a U.S. citizen as trustee.

In 1989, when laws affecting this category were passed,

any U.S. citizen could be the trustee of a QDOT trust or trust company. Provisions were later added requiring, in the case of trusts worth $2 million or more, a U. S. financial institution or trust company to serve as trustee - perhaps not a good scenario for the wealthy estate holder who wishes to leave an estate or business to a non-citizen spouse and leave that spouse with control over the funds or the business.

A problem for the surviving spouse can arise, for example, when his or her assets are not the type that can be efficiently handled by a trust company such as income-generating real estate or special property. In such a case, a trust may actually cause a great deal of discomfort or even hostility between the surviving spouse and the appointed trust company. The case would be even more difficult for the spouse if there were no trust, perhaps, leaving the non-citizen widow or widower to pay estate tax of as much as 38%-50% of the estate value over $625,000 to the IRS within nine months of the bequeathing spouse's death. Without a suitable plan, this tax may have to be paid at the cost of liquidating a family business or other assets at fire-sale prices. In short, whether for financial or cultural reasons or simply because they prefer to be in control of their own assets, many spouses are uncomfortable with their money being managed by a large impersonal financial institution. The Family Partnership can be used to gain some control over such a situation.

A Case in Point.

In order to illustrate how a Family Partnership can alleviate many of above-mentioned difficulties, we're going to establish a hypothetical case which will demonstrate the various options a surviving non-U.S. citizen spouse might consider.

Let's assume that the assets were transferred to a QDOT trust and that the estate is over $2 million which would require a corporate trustee. Further, let's say that the assets themselves were first contributed to one or more Limited Partnerships in exchange for Limited Partnership interests, which by their very nature, prohibit control of Partnership activities by Limited Partners and, as in this case, the corporate trustee who is holding only a Limited Partnership interest.

For illustration, suppose a U.S. citizen was married to a non-U.S. citizen and they were co-owners of a business and all their wealth was tied up in this business that operates various hotel properties, each with debt and mortgages but with a combined equity of $6,000,000. Further, let's assume that their plan was to continue to add to their hotel chain using the equity and the debt to further grow the business.

Next, the U.S. citizen spouse and co-owner of the properties dies. If in the ensuing nine month period, the surviving non-citizen spouse chooses to be become a U.S. citizen, they are entitled to an unlimited deduction regarding the estate and would, thereby, pay no estate tax. If, however, this is not feasible or desirable, other complexities of the law would have to be quickly dealt with by the surviving non-citizen spouse. For instance, in order to avoid the massive - upwards of $2 million in this case - estate tax which would be due within nine months of their death, the non-U.S. citizen spouse would have to contribute one-half interest in the hotel properties into a Qualified Domestic Trust with a U.S. citizen or trust company as trustee.

Under this option and from that point forward, the surviving non-U.S. spouse would have to involve and seek the approval of the trust company in the day-to-day affairs and management of the hotel business. Understanding that the trust company has a right to refrain from assisting in any new acquisitions or loans, this situation could easily stagnate the growth of the business, perhaps leaving the surviving spouse in even greater difficulty.

If the surviving non-U.S. spouse in this unfortunate circumstance chose to sell the properties, a massive capital gains tax might result in addition to the possibility that up to one-half of the sale proceeds would be held by the corporate trustee and could be invested in a manner not suitable to him. On the other hand, if the surviving non-U.S. spouse elected to hold the properties, he would have to continue to deal with the trustee on daily details of the business, all the while paying handsome trustee fees and costs for the privilege.

Enter the Family Partnership.

If a Family Partnership had been included in this estate plan before the first death occurred and the above-discussed properties had been contributed to it, the situation facing the non-U.S. citizen surviving spouse could have been considerably improved in a number of ways. When the first death occurred, the estate which now contained the properties contributed in exchange for Limited Partnership interests would have been valued at a discount. This discount might have been enough to reduce the estate to under the $2 million threshold, which eliminates the requirement that the trustee be a U.S. trust company. If this calculated discount had been sufficient to exempt the QDOT trust from requiring an institutional trustee, a friendly U.S. citizen family member son, daughter, or friend - could then have been selected to serve as trustee.

If the taxable estate remained over $2 million, a corporate U.S. trustee would have to be appointed. However, the corporate trustee would have little or no influence over the family's business as stipulated in the Limited Partnership agreement including the fact that the trustee would not be allowed to participate in the management of the properties since the properties are owned by the Partnership. Therefore, there will be little or no opportunity for the trustee to inhibit the growth of the business or having day-to-day conflicts with the management (surviving spouse).

The trustee would receive only the net income of the Limited Partnership interest which the trust estate owns. It then must turn around and distribute the income to the surviving spouse. In short, the use of a Family Partnership can restore control of an estate and businesses to the family of the people who created the assets in the first place.

In Summary.

We have seen how the Family Partnership is of enormous benefit in the estate planning process. In the above example, if the Partnership had been created before the first death, it could have saved estate taxes, administrative costs and many of the frustrations and intrusions of having to deal with a corporate trust department.

In addition, the Partnership could have been arranged to allow and facilitate the use of the annual $100,000 exclusion that a U.S. citizen can transfer annually to his or her non-citizen spouse, this sum replacing unlimited transfers that married U.S. citizens can transfer between themselves.

While estate planning for non-U.S. citizens can be complicated and holds its share of pitfalls, especially in the event that the foreign national spouse chooses not to become a U.S. citizen, a Family Partnership can be utilized to permit control of assets by the surviving spouse, defer the estate tax, reduce the estate tax through valuation discounts and perhaps eliminate appointing a corporate trust of the QDOT assets and, thus, protect the non-citizen spouse's interests.

CHAPTER
4

Advance Financial Planning for Middle America.

In light of today's financial standards, one does not have to be a member of the Walton family, a famous neurosurgeon or even someone married to a foreign national to find themselves in need of the many benefits of a Family Partnership. In actuality, the Family Partnership will become an increasingly important financial vehicle in light of certain economic factors such as a quickly appreciating stock market, the current high cost of housing and the fact that many middle-class American families are, as a result of these conditions, being forced into higher income tax brackets which puts cash flow and, eventually, estate tax demands on their lives and estates.

In addition, the Family Partnership will merit even greater consideration by parents of the next generation due to their continued high rate of divorce and the resulting concerns about how to keep a family's money safe in light of the statistically probable divorce of any involved children. However, even less critical but equally-important financial circumstances can encourage the use of the Family Partnership.

Let's take the story of our friend Bob as a case in point. When we last met, Bob reported that he was doing just fine. His three children all seemed reasonably well-adjusted and were growing nicely, his professional practice was appreciating and it appeared that he had appropriately arranged his finances and investments so as to save taxes and adequately provide for his family's future. Yes, things seemed to be going along just fine for Bob and his wife.

Next we heard, things had taken a surprising turn. One Tuesday afternoon, Bob returned home earlier than usual after coaching Little League for his youngest son and found himself in need of a key to the closet where his oldest son kept his drum set. He went into his son's room to retrieve the key and, as he was leaving the room, his son entered, giving them an opportunity to chat about the day's activities. While talking, Bob casually looked down and noticed a number of videotapes from rock n' roll bands as well as a meeting planner from a local resort hotel on his son's desk.

Suddenly inquisitive about his son's activities, Bob looked up and asked, "What's going on, planning something for school?" Then Bob's most senior son answered, "Actually, I've been meaning to tell you and Mom about this. I want to throw a big party for my 21st birthday, you know, with a live band and all, maybe even fly in the whole family for the weekend. It'll be just great, don't you think?"

Bob thought as fast as he could and then asked, "Son, that all sounds great but I'm wondering - just how are you planning to pay for this huge event?" Much to his shock, Bob's pride and joy had an answer. "You know, Dad, that money you've been putting away for me since I was in grade school? Well, I've decided I'm going to use that for my party." In order to prevent Bob's apparent near faint, his son threw an arm around the old boy and said, "Gee, Dad, don't worry - I wasn't going to spend it all!"

Nonetheless, with serious concerns over the possible ill-fated use of the nearly $100,000 in each of three custodian accounts he had been funding for his children, Bob wasted no time in paying a visit to his lawyer the very next day. His only order of business was to find a way to protect the funds that he had put aside for his family from misuse. And, once again, the Family Partnership saved the day.

Among the alternatives that where discussed at that meeting, Bob's lawyer suggested the establishment of a Family Limited Partnership which required the immediate contribution of certain of Bob's own assets. With that much in place and, in order to provide the all-important protection of family funds that Bob sought, Bob, acting as custodian under the Uniform Transfers to Minors Act (UTMA), then made contributions of each custodian account to the Partnership. As part of this agreement, each child would be receiving a Limited Partnership interest which would represent the value of the custodian account contributed.

The Partnership interest was then registered under their state's respective Uniform Transfers to Minor Act account and, when each child reached the age 21, the Partnership interest would be re-registered in that child's name alone. Thus, the child will receive value in the form of Limited Partnership interests for the transfers made by their custodian under the Uniform Transfers to Minors Act. The beauty of this plan is in the fact that it allowed Bob to continue to freely gift his children the money he wanted to put aside for them while safe-guarding and maintaining authority over these assets.

Then how, you might ask, will Bob determine the amount and the appropriate time to actually give the money over to his sons and his daughter? Bob gets to make that decision at his discretion because he is the General Partner of the Family Limited Partnership. As General Partner, Bob is at all times in command of the what happens to the funds including whether he distributes the money or keeps it as income or principal. It could be said that this plan effectively averted what might have developed into a lasting and major family controversy and led to further safeguards surrounding the family's financial assets.

Expanded Use and Benefits - Age 21 to 40.

There is, however, an even more far-reaching benefit of the Family Partnership for holding the moneys set aside for the use of minor children after age 21. Let's suppose that, years later, Bob's son - now past 21 - gets married, wants to buy a house and start a family. If Dad had transferred his portfolio to the son outright at age 21 as was the pre-Family Partnership plan, the son would now be in a position to use these funds for the down payment on a house. Should that have happened and, after a period of time, the marriage failed, some of that equity might likely have fallen into the hands of the child's ex-spouse, most likely, making Bob a doubly unhappy guy.

Fortunately, in this case because the Family Partnership had been executed to prevent the cost of that birthday extravaganza, a Partnership loan could have been made for the down payment on the house, thus, protecting the son's portfolio and providing multiple benefits such as:

1) By use of a loan from the Partnership, the son would have begun saving money as his mortgage payment to the Partnership was, in reality, part of his own money, the rest belonging to his brother, sister and parents, and

2) If there should have been a divorce, any equity that had been placed in the house by the Partnership would remain in the family as it was loaned to the son rather then gifted.

3) The Family Partnership will spread income tax from the father's higher tax bracket to the children's lower brackets. Then we note that the son's arrival at age 21 does not cause his tax bracket to suddenly equal his Dad's. Hence, until those tax brackets are the same, it pays for income and estate tax reasons to continue transferring more to the children. Yet, with most Transfers to Minors Act accounts, the transfers stop at 21 when the parent suddenly realizes they are totally out of control and must give the money to the child. With a Family Partnership in place, however, the income spreading can go on as long as it is profitable with no loss of control on behalf of the gifting parent. In other words, as tax brackets change, the investments in the Partnership can change as well as the mix of partners even allowing the children to start including their offspring in the mix.

In Summary.

In summary, we learned how hardworking families can suddenly find themselves in need of advance planning and can use a Family Limited Partnership to control their assets while continuing to make transfers to their kids and avoiding any pitfalls which might arise form the frequently used, but largely misunderstood custodian accounts for minors. The results include saved income and estate taxes, some protection from divorces and control staying with Dad, the General Partner.

Advanced Planning Pointer # 3

Contributing Securities Portfolios to the Family Partnership.

IRS guidelines discourage the contribution of certain negotiable securities to an existing portfolio under conditions which work to avoid the taxation of unrealized gain on those securities. What this means, in brief, is that you are not allowed to diversify your holdings by contributing your securities tax free to a Limited Partnership. The regulations are quite clear and they provide several case studies of what can be done and what cannot be done. However, with proper advice, it is possible to accomplish this goal without breaking the Internal Revenue Service rules. Please see Appendix I for further help on this issue.

CHAPTER
5

The Guide to Life
Insurance Ownership.

O f all the financial products ever created, life insurance is probably the most misunderstood, misused and under-utilized. While it is not our purpose to correct the misconceptions or misuses associated with this product, we include life insurance in our Family Partnership discussion because it can be used economically and profitably as a legitimate and valuable part of an estate plan. Used in conjunction with the Family Partnership, life insurance can create greater net worth for a family. With the goal of understanding how that can happen, let's start with a look at the general benefits of insurance.

Permanent life insurance - cash value or whole life insurance - is simply a guaranteed savings plan. The life insurance agreement states that an insuring company promises to pay a determined amount of money at the time of the insured's death or, as with some companies, when the insured reaches age 99. The insurance company also guarantees that, in the time period between the issuance of the policy and its pay out, any cash value or equity which exists in the policy can be borrowed by the owner without question or application.

Loans against the equity which accrue interest further offset the policy proceeds, therefore, making it financially wise to pay any interest on the loan annually. Policy loan interest is generally deductible if the loan proceeds are used for investment or business purposes. Irrespective of any loans, the death benefit or pay out is guaranteed as long as the policy remains in force, the death benefit reduced only by the amount of outstanding loans that have been made by the owner.

In most cases, the insurance policy also provides benefits such as premium payment continuation in the event of the disability of the insured. Some insuring companies even allow policy proceeds to be paid early if the insured is determined to be terminally ill. Other benefits of life insurance include the fact that the IRS does not tax the equity (cash value) for income tax purposes and, in many states, the cash value in such policies is completely exempt from creditor claims. Of course, life insurance is not the highest yielding investment in the world and was never intended to be, rather, its function is to guarantee a result. In this aspect, it is one of the best tax shelters available today due to the income tax-free death benefit and the tax-free availability of the funds including the growth they earn.

The guaranteed death benefit results in the proceeds becoming part of the owner's estate and subject to estate tax. Before we take a look at how life insurance can be set up more profitably to avoid heavy estate taxes through careful planning, let's get an understanding of the various ways in which life insurance ownership can be arranged.

Life Insurance Ownership Options.

In pure form, while there is no income tax levied on the death benefit, the value of insurance death proceeds are included in the taxable estate of the policy owner in the same manner as mutual funds, business interests, gold coins or other such assets. However, if the policy on the insured is owned by someone else or by some business entity, the death benefit may be excluded from the estate of the insured. This type of outside ownership can, thus, protect an estate from having assets sold at fire sale prices in order to pay tax which is due within nine months of an insured's death. Next, a look at a number of options and considerations for life insurance ownership.

Life Insurance Trust.

In one instance, let's assume that Dad forms a trust, appoints a trustee and has the trust buy a life insurance policy on his life. Each year Dad makes gifts to the trusts equal to the insurance premiums and the trust sends out a letter to each of the trust beneficiaries - most likely, the children - asking them if they want the money in cash or if they want to leave it in the trust. These letters are required because, in order to use the annual $10,000 per person gift tax exclusions, the gifts must be "gifts of a present interest" meaning the recipient must have the option of benefiting from the funds currently. The children, of course, are strongly advised by Dad not to request the money from the trustee but, instead, to leave it in the trust. The trust then uses the money to pay for the life insurance.

But, what happens if one year Dad and the children are not getting along and the they decide they'd rather spend their

$10,000 gifts rather than letting the trust keep the money? Well, the children have the option of doing just that. And, the result would be that Dad's plan to purchase the insurance through the trust to pay any estate tax would begin to weaken. This weakening could also happen if the life insurance is owned by the children rather than a trust, subjecting the cash value to the children's spending habits. In the event, however, that the owner-children are fiscally responsible and that they outlive the insured, this form of ownership is fine and can work without risk of the policy lapsing.

Let's then consider an economic factor that might arise when determining how best to assign life insurance policy ownership. As we have already mentioned, cash equity in a whole life policy is available for investments and other business or personal needs including emergencies. This liquidity is a real benefit of an insurance policy and should be considered in determining whether the insured should be the owner and have this cash value available for other uses or emergencies or if a trust should own the policy and take the cash out of play.

In deciding whether or not to commit the cash value of an insurance policy to an irrevocable trust rather than to individual ownership, consider what impact available cash values might have on a business, perhaps, providing money for capital improvements or inventory expansion. If, for example, the money in a life insurance policy can be borrowed for 7% interest rather than the 15% or greater interest a bank or leasing company might charge, it might be prudent to use the equity available to do that kind of work. Or, if a life insurance policy is earning interest dividends at the rate of 6% and a loan from this fund would result in 7% interest, a net savings of 8% on the borrowed sum would be realized. Additionally, the insurance stays in force as the premiums are paid and the insurance company continues to guarantee that funds will be available to pay the IRS when the insured dies.

Typically, by using an irrevocable trust, the option of using the money in other ways is lost. While the irrevocable trust does its job well of protecting the estate by disallowing any trustees from taking risk with the cash in the policy; thus, protecting the trust beneficiaries and keeping the full proceeds out of the estate, the trust has other limitations and associated costs such as those preventing the best present use of the policy's equity.

One of the most serious restrictions of the irrevocable life insurance trust has to do with the amount of insurance it can hold. Generally, the face value of a life insurance policy assigned to such a trust is determined by the annual premium that is calculated on the basis of the $10,000 per year per child gift limitation. The insurance trust can prove limiting when, for instance, there is only one child involved that would set the maximum premium allowable at $10,000, this could possibly result in the corresponding amount of insurance being insufficient to cover the death benefit needed to meet the estate tax.

Let's see just how far the Family Partnership can go in conjunction with life insurance towards providing outstanding options for protecting a family's estate.

The Family Partnership: A No-Limit Solution.

The Family Partnership and ownership of life insurance seems to offer the ideal combination most especially, as we saw in our first chapter study of the Walton family, when dealing with highly appreciating property such as Wal-Mart stock.

The life insurance contract, very much like the shares of Wal-Mart which appreciated during Sam Walton's tenure, appreciates over time, then performs at peak upon the death of the insured.

In the case of life insurance, there is no doubt that - if premiums are paid - the policy will appreciate and, eventually, cash out at a determined face value. What's more, any appreciation is tax free for income tax purposes, therefore, making the life insurance contract a powerful financial vehicle which is well-suited to being held by a Family Partnership.

The Mechanics of Life Insurance and Family Partnerships.

The Family Partnership can receive as a contribution from the insured - a Partner - an existing life insurance policy or buy new ones on any Partner's life. While the beneficiary of such a life insurance contract must be the Partnership, there is no limit on how much life insurance a Partnership can own. It is only limited by the ability of the insurance companies to issue it and the Partnership's supply of funds to pay the premiums.

A parent, for example, who is worth $25,000,000 and has one child, might choose to set up a Partnership and have it buy a $12,500,000 life insurance policy on their life. The value of the insurance is based on an approximation of the amount of estate tax which will be due upon the insured death. Next, the parent contributes to the Partnership the necessary premiums that will be due to the life insurance company. Annually, in exchange for the contribution of such premiums, the parent receives an ownership interest in the

Partnership or Limited Partnership interest. In turn, the parent gives those Partnership interests to his only child as quickly as he is allowed, transferring $10,000 per year or even $635,000 the first year through his unified credit, then $10,000 each year thereafter.

Estate Tax Issues/Benefits.

When the parent dies, the life insurance company pays the $12,500,000 to the Partnership. The parent's estate, subject to estate tax on the value of the Partnership interest which the parent owed at the time of death, may be subject to a discount. In this example, an amount equal to his percentage of ownership in the Partnership from the insurance proceeds will be included in the parent's estate. This figure could be quite large or small depending on the size of the holdings but, in any event, it represents a disadvantage to the Family Partnership. While life insurance owned by an irrevocable trust is generally outside the estate, a Family Partnership is usually included to some degree, but the ultimate benefit of this trade off is maintained control which gives access to the cash values for Partnership purposes.

The Benefit of Control.

The question one must ultimately answer is - which is better, control and some estate taxes; or no control and no estate taxes? Certainly it's an individual preference but most people, especially business people, typically chose to retain control even in the event of some estate tax. The person who retains control of a Partnership that holds a business, for example, can then continue to access funds for growth or acquisitions. He could also choose to make a loan from the Partnership to his children for enough money to buy a house or start a business. In short, most people would rather retain control of their assets including the cash values in the life insurance policies until death.

Also note here that, as discussed in Advanced Planning Pointer # 2 in Chapter 2, the IRS is currently allowing gift and estate tax valuation discounts on transfers of Family Partnership interests. While we don't know if this will continue to be the case, let's see how things currently work. With an irrevocable Crummey Trust, the limitation of gifts for insurance premium is $10,000 per child per parent. Using the valuation discounts allowed for transfers of non-liquid Partnership interest and an assumed 30% discount, an annual exclusion of $14,286 could be expected. In other words, this same annual exclusion could purchase 42.86% more life insurance providing one more excellent reason to use a Family Partnership instead of a Irrevocable Life Insurance trust.

Note: Family Partnerships can, in some cases, be used to purchase life insurance contracts out of existing irrevocable life or Crummey Trusts. While such procedures are highly technical, they can, when correctly done, solve the lack of control issues which linger with irrevocable trusts.

In short, it is clear that having the life insurance policy on the General Partner or multiple Partners owned by the Family Partnership generates a wealth of planning opportunities which are not available with the irrevocable life insurance trust. The Family Partnership is a valuable option to be executed by competent counsel in planning an estate.

Advanced Planning Pointer #5
Transfer for Value Rules.

A transfer of value takes place when a life insurance policy is sold to someone who will receive the benefit on the death of the insured, an arrangement which could make the beneficiary liable for the payment of income tax or death proceeds. However, with regard to life insurance policies, the transfer for value rule does not consider it a transfer for value if the insured is a Partner of the Partnership which is receiving the policy. Therefore, the Family Partnership, where the insured is a partner can receive the policy and one day, the death benefit without income tax.

Advanced Planning Pointer #6
The Three Year Rule.

The pay out of the face value of a life insurance policy upon the death of the insured is most often quite a significant benefit to the estate of the insured. In response to this, the IRS has decreed that any policy which is given away within three years of the death of the insured is automatically recalled into the estate and, thus, made part of the estate for estate tax purposes. However, we believe that if properly structured, a Family Partnership can be the recipient of a contribution rather than a gift of life insurance and, thereby, cause the process to reside outside the three-year rule saving perhaps millions depending on the size and circumstances of the estate. Note: See TAM 9413045 wherein the IRS defines adequate consideration for the transfer of a policy to be equal to the cash values plus unearned premiums. Also IRC 2035(b)(1) which gives the exception to the rule for a sale in exchange for adequate and full consideration.

Advanced Planning Pointer #7
Incidences of Ownership.

The Internal Revenue Code and case law specify that if one has incidences of ownership on a policy when they die, then that policy is included in their estate. Incidences of ownership characteristics are defined in the Internal Revenue Code, but the exception that is applicable to this topic is that a Partner in a Partnership which owns a life insurance policy on the Partner's life and the Partnership is the beneficiary, then the Partner's estate only has to include the prorated value of that Partnership in such Partner's estate including the proceeds of death. This inclusion is before any applicable valuation discount.

CHAPTER 6

Financial Focus for Doctors, Professionals and Business Owners.

D octors, other professionals and successful business owners have similar tax and estate problems in that typically they are in high income tax brackets, frequently have substantial assets for investments and are concerned about both income and estate taxes, and about keeping their assets safe from any outside pressures. These kinds of financial pressures can come, not just from lawsuits, but from other outside sources such as the Internal Revenue Service, future ex-in-laws, or even spendthrift children who see the big earner as a source of funds. Therefore, advanced planning for such people is vitally important to keeping their assets intact, under their control and out of harm's way.

The Basic Savings of a Family Limited Partnership.

So, let's take the example of a couple - one of which is a

doctor, professional or business person - who sets up a Family Partnership and transfers property into it. In exchange, they receive 100% of the General Partnership interests and 100% of the Limited Partnership interests of the newly created Family Partnership. The General Partnership interests are the ones which control the Limited Partnership interests which have little control. Next, let's assume that this couple transfers a percentage of their Limited Partnership interest - not cash - to their children.

This removes equity from the estate and puts it in the estates of their children without giving them any power to control or manipulate such investments, provided the Partnership agreement is properly structured. In short, this transaction does not give the children any assets which are easy to sell or borrow money against. Rather, the assets are maintained in the same condition as when they were placed into the Partnership and the parents remain in control of any such assets.

The children will now have a portion of the taxable income from these assets in their - presumably - lower tax brackets which will result in income tax savings on those portions of the estate that have been transferred. Note: See Chapter 2 for a more thorough explanation of this scenario.

Now, because the equity has been transferred out of the parents' estate into the children's estates using the annual $10,000 exclusions, the taxable estate of the parents has been reduced by that amount and their estate tax will reflect a reduction of approximately $5,000 per transfer, per child. While this may not initially appear that substantial a savings, over time these $5,000 per year gifts to each child can, indeed, amount to considerable tax savings. In addition, through the receipt of substantial interest, dividends or rents, the children's estates will also continue to take on their share of the increased value.

Valuation discounts may also be considered as a way to move

money more quickly out of the parents' taxable estate using either evaluation discount as discussed in Chapter 2, Advanced Planning Pointer #2. In that event, substantial income and estate tax savings on the part of the family may be realized. Further, additional savings might be realized through the use of intangible tax or other nuisance tax savings as the Partnership may allow and as explained in Chapter 10.

In Summary.

In this example, we have saved income taxes by allowing our children in lower tax brackets to pay taxes on some income that otherwise would have been taxable in the parents' tax brackets. We have reduced our estate taxes by making small transfers of Limited Partnership interest to the children yet protected the estate in that the agreement prohibits the children from spending or consuming the transferred assets as they are being held by the Partnership.

Limited Partnerships Can Be Creditor Resistant.

One of the most unique and important characteristics of the Limited Partnership is that aspect which comes under the Revised Uniform Limited Partnership Act (RULPA) as it relates to dealing with creditors. Such creditors might include the Internal Revenue Service, lawsuit or other malpractice claimants, even a teenage child's car accident victim.

When the Partnership is set as a Limited Partnership under the Revised Uniform Limited Partnership Act which has been adopted by 49 states - except in Louisiana *(see questions 37-39)* - it possesses certain features under the law that automatically provides planning benefits. One such benefit is that such a Partnership cannot be broken or be disrupted by the creditors of any Partner or any group of Partners. Therefore, even if a Partner should be subject to a judgment claim, his or her interest in the Partnership cannot be attached or taken away. Please note that this protection pertains only to liabilities that originate from outside the Partnership as the Partnership and the General Partners are always subject to whatever liabilities they bring upon themselves in the course of Partnership business. This, of course, is reasonable as the General Partners control the Partnership, thus, makes any decisions that the Partnership would be obligated to regarding debt or performance of contractual obligations.

If the Partnership owns a piece of real estate and someone visiting that location falls, breaks a hip and, subsequently, sues the Partnership for negligence, the Partnership would have to defend itself against or be responsible for that claim. Under certain other circumstances, the Partnership can act to protect assets from similar types of threats. If, for example, the Partners own this same real estate and the General Partner is a surgeon who gets sued for malpractice, the Partnership prevents the malpractice claimant from taking any real estate held by the Partnership, thus protecting the surgeon from losing control of his assets.

Likewise, if real estate, or Exxon shares, or any other asset are held in the owner's name and a lawsuit is filed and lost, these assets can fall prey to confiscation by the successful claimant. If, instead, a Limited Partnership held title to that piece of land or shares of stock, creditors could not access such investments in satisfaction of any lawsuit claims. Rather, in the case of property that is held in a Limited Partnership, the creditor could receive from the court only something called a charging order, which allows a creditor to stand and receive whatever Partnership cash or assets would be paid out to the Partner against whom the creditor has a judgment. The creditor does not become a Partner in the Partnership nor can he vote his interests. The best he can do is simply stand in the way to receive whatever distributions that Limited Partner is due to receive. So, the Revised Uniform Limited Partnership Act protects all Partnerships including Investment Limited Partnerships and Business Limited Partnerships from creditors of the Partner for very good economic and business reasons. Let's look at another example of how this Act protects a Partnership.

Imagine that a Limited Partnership is registered by the Securities and Exchange Commission and set up to be sold nationwide raising $30 million in $10,000 Limited Partnerships units, in order to buy an apartment complex in Daytona Beach, Florida. Next, let's assume that the offering is complete, the money is raised and the property in Daytona is bought and is operating successfully.

Sometime later, one of the Limited Partners from California gets sued and the case is not decided in his favor; which opens the door for the creditor. This creditor could now be standing on the Partnership's doorstep trying to force the sale of the Daytona property in order to pay off their liability judgment. Here's where the charging orders are in place to protect the Partnership and the other Limited Partners that might be damaged if such a property had to be forced into early sale.

Under the law, the only thing a judgment creditor can do is go to court with his judgment and get a charging order against that Limited Partner's interest. The Partnership is safe and can continue its business. If and when it does make a distribution, the creditor would be entitled to only the amount of his judgment as it would come out of that Partner's distribution.

It is important to remember here that it is up to the General Partner of the Limited Partnership to determine what, if any, distributions are made. Should the General Partner, believing that the money is better invested inside the Partnership, decide against distributing any money or if no money is available, the holder of the charging order receives nothing. Thus, the creditor is basically left to sit and wait for any distributions that might be made by and at the whim of the General Partner.

In short, Partnership law allows the Partnership agreement to contain the provision that distribution of Partnership income or principal be made only upon the decision of the General Partner. This provision coupled with the law allowing a judgment creditor of a Partner to receive a charging order against that Partner's distribution when and if it is made results in the creditor receiving nothing in the event that the General Partner decides to make no distribution.

An Aside.

Please note that all Limited Partners must be treated equally relative to their percentage in the Partnership. A General Partner, for example, cannot refuse to make a distribution to one Limited Partner then make distributions of profit or principal to others. However, the General Partner may elect to not make any distributions of income or principal to any Partner yet provide secured or unsecured loans to selected Limited Partners, presumably and logically, those Partners which are financially sound.

To the extent that a Limited Partner may need money for some legitimate purpose, the General Partner can lend them cash in exchange for an interest-bearing note to the benefit of the Limited Partnership and without any adverse consequence. It might even be possible for the General Partner to loan money to the Partner who has the judgment against them as the property inside the Partnership cannot be sold off, segregated or otherwise given away to creditors. Also, if a Limited Partnership is set up to defraud creditors, a judge could overturn this charging order protection.

In Summary.

From the creditor's point of view, the outlook is that he or she must hire and pay attorneys' fees along with any relevant costs and then wage a long battle in court in order to gain judgment against someone who has a Partnership interest in a Limited Partnership. The creditor must be prepared to face the fact that judgments are not easy to come by given the time and money expended to obtain a decision from the court. Even after a creditor has attained a judgment, he typically has to depose the person against whom he has the judgment in order to determine what assets are owned. If, in addition to a Limited Partnership interest, there are sufficient other non-exempt assets available, the creditor will take those first. However, if the only other substantial asset that the debtor has is a Limited Partnership interest then the creditor is now faced with getting a charging order and waiting for that Limited Partnership interest to pay him his money.

More Protection Against Creditors.

As a Partnership pays no tax on its income, the tax ramifications of whatever profits it earns are passed on to the Partners prorata. Therefore, if the Partnership earns $100,000 in net taxable income per year and a Partner owns 10%, he or she will have to pay tax on $10,000, 10% of $100,000. The tax on this amount will be in the Partner's tax bracket and will be due whether cash is received or not. And, as for the creditor who is not a Partner, the IRS might have some unpleasant news. In 1977, a ruling was stated that, since a creditor is getting the economic benefit of the Partnership operations during the time period in which a charging order is held, the creditor, rather than the Partner, should be responsible for the income tax. This Revenue Ruling #77-176 means that creditors who file charging orders must pay tax on phantom income that can result even when a Partnership earns income but the General Partnership elects to make no distribution.

Time for Another Reality Check.

Despite all the benefits that charging orders and revenue rulings might bestow on the Partnership agreement, it's important to note that they do not - singularly or jointly -prevent lawsuits. Further, Partnerships are not shielded from the courts or subpoenas and they do not replace appropriate insurance coverage, which is designed to protect against specific claims. However, the Partnership can act as one further significant line of defense against a stubborn, well-financed and well-represented creditor.

Other Family Partnership Options.

One of the other considerations of Limited Partnerships is that they require capital to be effective. In order to save on income tax, money or assets must be available to be turned into transferable Partnership interests for children or other beneficiaries. When such funds are available, the

Family Partnership can provide an additional backdrop of some creditor protection while the gifts of the Partnership interest saves substantial estate taxes. There is, however, another use of the Partnership to be considered in the tax-saving effort.

Let's start with the assumption that almost every business or professional practice holds some type of assets - computers, desks, chairs, sometimes even medical testing equipment, X-ray machines and the like. Here's what could happen if a second Partnership was structured for the purpose of acquiring all types of assets from a corporation with an arrangement to lease them back to the corporation. Some results might be:

1) Taxable income would be moved, for example, from the business owner, professional, or doctor to their children.

2) Assets would be moved in the same way to save estate tax.

3) Positive cash flow would be generated that could be used for college educations and the like.

4) The balance sheet of the corporation would be cleaned up to allow for admittance of new business Partners, etc.

5) Security interest would be placed on other assets of the corporation, including receivables, in order to forestall attachment by future unknown creditors.

At this point, a second non-investment Partnership could be set up to purchase any of the business equipment through a purchase money note which would require little capital.

With the amount of capital relatively small, the parent could transfer all the Limited Partnership interests to their children almost instantaneously. This would result in Partnership profits being taxed in the younger generations tax brackets.

The Lease Agreement.

In this transaction, the lease agreement is the most critical factor in achieving the most advantageous savings. For this purpose, any such lease agreement must be structured as a commercial lease in favor of the leasing company which is the new Equipment Limited Partnership. Typical provisions for such an agreement might include:

1) Lease payment to be fixed at a high rate in keeping with the type of equipment involved.

2) Partnership to provide new capital to the business or corporation on short notice, which allows the lease to be included at a higher stand-by credit rate.

3) The Equipment Leasing Partnership will reimburse the corporation for ordinary maintenance on the equipment providing it is billed within 60 days of performance of said maintenance services.

4) In the event of default by the corporation, the Equipment Leasing Partnership gets to claim:

   a. All future lease payments, as equipment is usually specialized.

   b. A substantial default penalty.

   c. Possession of the equipment.

On taking the above steps, here's what could ensue. The sale of the business equipment to the Equipment Leasing

Partnership would be made with appropriate publications under the bulk sales rules and from that point forward the corporation would write a lease check to the Partnership each month. If the Partnership bought the equipment using a note, the Partnership would write back a note payment check. Appropriate security statements are filed securing the corporations other assets, including receivables. Due to the excess of the lease payments over the note payment, the Partnership would generate positive cash flow and remove taxable income from the corporation in favor of its Partners, primarily, the children.

Should a disaster such as a large medical malpractice claim befall the business or the family, the corporation would probably default on its lease obligation to the Partnership as it might well be spending all of its funds in defending itself. When the corporation defaults, the Leasing Partnership could then come in and regain possession of all the equipment as well as any other significant assets including accounts receivable. While the Partnership might not acquire title to all of these assets, whatever it did acquire could possibly protect the integrity of the practice or business interest for a restart at some future date and, thereby, protect the family from a possible financial collapse.

In Summary.

Limited Partnerships have significant creditor resistant features including protecting assets from liabilities caused by other investment entities or professional liabilities. Partnerships can be creatively designed to hold leasing programs which further protect an estate by assuming liability for any equipment or lawsuit judgments thus leaving the original assets intact for the use of the family for college education or other aspects of estate and retirement planning. Any resulting profits can be accumulated, invested or paid out in accordance with the dictates of the General Partner.

Advanced Planning Pointer # 8.

The Creditor vs. Estate Planning.

When it comes to the doctor, professional or small business owner with regard to advance planning in Florida, the following are typically concerns. 1) In order to achieve proper estate planning, it is advantageous for each of a married couple to have $625,000 (grown to $1,000,000 in 2007) worth of assets. This is usually accomplished by setting up two separate individual living trusts and transferring the $625,000 into each so that when they die, the $625,000 lifetime exclusion is fully utilized which will result in estate tax savings of over $192,800 per person. When this is done in Florida and many other states, the $1.25 million dollars worth of assets that have been removed from the couple's joint names are regarded as owned by only one of the spouses and no longer joint property. This adds a layer of creditor protection as, again, in Florida and certain other states, tenancy-by-the-entireties property is exempted from the judgment creditors of one of the people. Once removed,the property, it is no longer considered tenancy-by-the-entireties, hence, loses that protection.

To further understand how this works, let's take the example of a doctor who is sued for malpractice relating to his medical practice but whose wife is not responsible for any such claims unless she can be brought in as a co-defendant due to involvement in the practice. Should the doctor lose the suit and have a judgment against him, the assets that he and his wife own jointly will not be attached. However, it is important to note that, if they have a proper estate plan and their assets are separate in order to save the $192,800 in estate taxes as discussed above, those $625,000 worth of assets are at risk of being taken by the creditor as they are in the doctor's name only. In fact, a living trust is of no use in this particular scenario.

This is an interesting dilemma for a good lawyer to face. The question is which to plan for, the estate tax savings or the maybe- creditor? If a plan is set up to protect against the creditor, the potential loss is $192,800 in increased estate tax due to the loss of the unified credit. But, if the attorney sets the plan up to save the $192,800 then there might be the potential loss of $625,000 in creditor claims.

There are, of course, other concerns. Let's next suppose that all the assets are put in the name of the doctor's spouse, as the spouse is less likely to be the target of a lawsuit. This is all well and good if the doctor has no concern for the possibility of arriving home one day to an empty home and checkbook. On the other hand, people in these types of situations might feel that the separation of assets into two equal parts is more likely to cause discord in the relationship or even divorce.

One solution for these types of dilemmas is a Family Partnership not only for its tax saving features but for its unique creditor-resistant properties in dealing with otherwise non-exempt properties.

Note: Please remember that a Family Limited Partnership is not exempt from creditors as an IRA or life insurance might be. Family Limited Partnerships are defensive measures only.

Advance Planning Pointer # 9
Default on a Lease.

For protection, a Partnership can capture receivables if a business stops making lease payments, but this is a standby transaction and it must be understood that there could be fairly severe income tax consequences. Should such a situation occur, any adverse tax consequences would have to be viewed as part of the investment of protecting ongoing business.

While it is probable, in the case of default on a lease transaction, that any creditors of the business will not be pleased to see substantial assets of the business being retained by the family members via a Family Partnership, these benefits may likely be defended as the Partnership which is set up for estate planning can also carry this type of creditor resistance. However, as with any dealings with the legal system, it is wise to have appropriate legal counsel.

CHAPTER
7

Getting the Best of Medicaid and Other Suggestions for the Aged.

It is not untypical to find aging people who are faced with the difficult choice of preparing for the possibilities of their own older years versus protecting their estate so it can be passed on intact to a spouse or children. On one hand, an aging spouse may desire to plan their estate in such a way that, even if he should have to be confined to a nursing home at the high cost of anywhere from $3,500 to $5,000 per month, his wife would have sufficient funds to live on, thereby, maintaining her customary standard of living. While his wife may share these concerns, she may have an equal desire to protect this same estate for their children.

There has been a noticeable shift in the collective attitudes of our country's seniors regarding the payment of nursing home costs. More often than in the past, elderly people are willing to take advantage of available government assistance for the payment of nursing home costs. It is quite clear that people increasingly feel that their contributions to Social Security and other tax agencies should entitle them to freely use Medicaid and other such benefits for which they are legally eligible. This trend is, undoubtedly, growing in proportion to the increasingly high cost of managed care.

Overall, clients have two goals in this area. First, older couples wish to insure the preservation of adequate resources towards any necessary costs should they become private pay patients in a skilled nursing facility. The second goal is to qualify as early as possible for Medicaid so as to avoid paying the high cost of skilled care and, thus, preserve the majority of the estate which is to be passed on to any children.

As to the moral implications of this type of planning, an older gentleman whose net worth was approximately $250,000 and whose wife was in a nursing home that was costing $4,700 per month shared an interesting thought when he pointed out that, if the $4,700 per month he was paying represented income or estate taxes, there would be no discussion regarding any moral dilemmas in planning to reduce such taxes. He was correct.

The law provides for planning options which help people legally avoid unnecessary taxes and it's the astute person who makes himself familiar enough with these options to use them to save costs. The countering point could also be made that income and estate taxes are for the common good and it is impossible to determine how much of that good one individual or one family is entitled to consume. As it is relatively easy to determine how much an individual or family consumes in a given nursing home situation, the question then becomes is it right for a person to deny that burden by using the law to avoid consuming a family's unique reserves to pay for this individual burden?

While this is a question individuals must answer for themselves, we believe that the legislature will, ultimately, address this issue by making Medicaid benefits more difficult to access in the case of adequate estates. In the case of the client who initiated this discussion, the decision was made in favor of what he perceived as the first duty to his family. Therefore, within legal limits and the intent of the law, this man's goal was to save whatever assets he could for his own and his wife's pre-Medicaid nursing home costs, for his children and his grandchildren's education funding.

That being this client's decision, let's look at a brief overview of the Florida law in this area in order to determine what this man's options were in accomplishing his goals.

Florida Medicaid Laws in Brief.

Without going into an in-depth analysis of Medicaid eligibility in general or even specific state requirements, which can be obtained from one's attorney, we can cover the two-prong test for Medicaid eligibility in consideration of benefits for residence in an assisted living, or skilled nursing care facility, or a nursing home. The first test is income-based, the second asset-based.

For example, in Florida, the income-base for eligibility is $1,352 per person with an exempted property amount of not more than $75,000 if married or $2,000 in non-exempt property for a single person. Exempted property consists of each state's definition of property excluded from this computation, normally your primary residence, your automobile and personal property.

If the two-prong test is met, Medicaid laws allow a person to make gifts of property on a monthly basis as long as such gifts do not exceed the state's established monthly cost for a private pay patient in a nursing home facility. The above rules mean that you can convert non-exempt property into exempt property and, thereby, become eligible for Medicaid. A few examples follow.

Example 1

If you are single and have $200,000 in cash but do not own a residence, you could spend the $200,000 on a home and, thereby, remove the $200,000 from non-exempt asset or cash status and convert it into the exempt asset of primary residence. Note: The planning process would have to include the cash consideration of maintenance and taxes on that home.

Example 2

Under the same above-mentioned circumstance, one could also purchase a car with the cash assets and still be eligible for Medicaid. In this scenario, one must consider the investment characteristics of an automobile including payments for insurance, maintenance, storage and upkeep.

Example 3

Let's take the case of a married woman with that same $200,000 whose husband is in a nursing home. The spouse would not be eligible for Medicaid because the joint, non-exempt assets would be more than the allowable $75,000.

However, their $200,000 could disappear off the balance sheet forever with the purchase of an immediate annuity which shows no cash value but pays a monthly sum for the rest of the purchaser's life.

This would work primarily because the rules for Medicaid eligibility ignore the non-confined spouse's separate income, but pays attention to her assets at the time of qualification for eligibility, hence, the above strategy is to remove assets but increase income. Should the spouse die soon after purchasing the annuity, however, the insurance company benefits and the family loses. An option that might work to avoid this outcome would be for the non-confined spouse to purchase an immediate annuity for a guaranteed number of years which would allow her to name beneficiaries who would receive the monthly income if she dies before the contract expires. Note: While some of these annuities can be variable in nature, most are very low-yielding.

Example 4

Now let's look at a case in which both the husband and wife are expected, at some future time to both go into a nursing home. This couple has $100,000 jointly held and additional exempt assets all of which they desire to keep under their own control. There are two primarily factors we need to address here. The first is that this couple has in excess of the $75,000 permitted in non-exempt assets for a couple. Additionally, if one of them should die, the level of non-exempt assets allowable in order for the survivor to qualify for Medicaid eligibility drops to $2,000.

One solution that could work towards preserving this

couple's assets to the maximum extent while maintaining Medicaid eligibility is for the non-confined spouse to make qualifying transfers to children - or selected others - equal to the monthly statutory amount. For the purpose of this discussion, we will use the monthly statutory amount of $3,500 per month. Note: The rationale for this law is that a person should be able to spend his or her money - at the nursing home rate - with family and friends prior to entering a skilled care facility.

In this instance, the couple could simply begin making qualifying transfers of $7,000 per month to their children or to a Family Partnership which is owned by the children. This plan, perhaps in conjunction with variations as discussed above, would over approximately fourteen months remove the $100,000 worth of assets from availability for any future nursing home expenditures - that is, $7,000 per month times 14 months equaling $98,000. At the end of this time period, the parents would be left with exempted assets and would qualify for Medicaid as soon as they needed it.

However, a gift of any amount over the established monthly private pay cost - the $3,500 used in the example above - would cause the parent to become ineligible to receive Medicaid benefits until the passage of a certain amount of time. This time period would be represented by the shorter of 1) the result of dividing the amount of the gift by the private pay monthly amount or 2) thirty-six months or sixty months if the prior figure is changed by the legislature or if a trust is used.

This is called the Medicaid look-back rule which simply means that the single parent who gave his children a gift of $100,000 and the next day applied for Medicaid would find himself ineligible and would have to wait thirty-six months to reapply. The Family Partnership can, however, be used to help a single parent or couple preserve their estate for nursing home costs, while insuring the pass along of their estate to family and heirs of the Family Partnership.

Once again, let's see how this would work. The couple or single parent establishes a Family Partnership, contributing all non-exempt assets to the Partnership either in bulk or slowly as described in the $7,000 per month schedule above. The Partnership then makes a gift of 99% of the limited interests to the children retaining the 1% General Partnership interest which would allow the parents to control the Partnership.

If, instead, the money was simply gifted to children or heirs, very different circumstances could arise. If this were the case and in the event that the gifting parent had to go into a nursing home prior to the thirty-six months time period, he or she would be required to pay as a private patient. Here's where the problems would begin as the parent is now without funds to pay the monthly nursing home cost as a private pay patient, especially if Social Security and pension money would not suffice. This might cause the parent to have to turn back to the children for financial assistance. Whereas with a Partnership all aspects of financial dealings have been pre-arranged, in this outright gift-giving scenario serious problems could arise if a child dies, divorces or gets into financial trouble before or while the parent needs support.

The Family Partnership eliminates these possibilities by keeping the assets in the parent's control. In fact, many people use a Partnership arrangement even if they have only one, totally trusted child in order to take advantage of all the benefits such as the creditor-resistant factors, intangible tax exclusions and valuation discounts. Ultimately, the Family

Partnership provides protection and peace of mind to the parents who want to be certain that their assets will not be spent, thereby, remaining available to pay for necessary private nursing care prior to the thirty-six month period. Finally, it's important to note that Medicaid planning is controversial and complicated and should be supervised by competent counsel.

Note: If a Medicaid application is turned down because assets were gifted away within the 36 months - or the shorter time period, if applicable - the waiting period may begin anew at 36 months from the date of your application.

CHAPTER 8

Divorce and Family Financial Affairs.

Years ago, it was not uncommon for a spouse who was thinking of getting a divorce to transfer mutually-held property into a Limited Partnership, nominating himself as General and Limited Partner and his wife as a Limited Partner. Subsequent to the Partnership setup, the husband would file for divorce and suggest that, as a property settlement, the wife keep her 50% interest in the Partnership and he would keep his 49% Limited Partnership interest along with the controlling 1% General Partnership interest. Basically and with other issues aside, this 50/50 split of marital property looked like an equitable arrangement but this was, of course, far from true as the wife had no control over the operation of the Partnership nor its distributions.

After the divorce, the husband might chose to stop distributions to the spouse in order to use the funds for

Partnership purposes which might cut off a source of income that the wife depended on for living expenses. Causing further trauma was the fact that, as we discussed in dealing with the creditors in Chapter 6, the lack of distribution or non-payment of the income would not reduce the wife's obligation to pay income taxes on the funds allocated as her proportion of Partnership income. Instead of being provided with an income, the wife was now in ownership of an asset which couldn't be sold on the open market, yet was annually costing her considerable sums of tax money.

When this became an untenable situation for the wife, the former husband would approach her, offering to buy her Limited Partnership interest at a discount to their nominal value. For instance, if the interest represented 50% ownership in a Partnership that held $1,000,000 in assets, her Partnership interests would have a nominal value of $500,000. But, the former husband might offer her a cash price of $200,000 - or less - for those interests. Should the wife accept, the husband could then purchase her interests at the agreed upon price. To the extent the purchase price is less than $500,000, he has recaptured some of the wealth that would otherwise have been lost in the divorce. In short, he gives his wife $500,000 in assets then buys them back for $200,000. There have, in fact, been actual cases structured along these lines where because the ex-spouse badly needed funds for living and to cover income taxes that the purchase price to the wife was a mere 12 cents on the dollar.

However, in covering the topic of divorce and finance, it should be noted that judges today have quite a wide latitude when it comes to making settlements and, even when a Family Partnership is used to plan for in anticipation of divorce, divorce attorneys and future ex-spouses have become familiar enough with the dramatic advantages of being the General Partner in a Family Limited Partnership that these types of situations seldom occur. In fact, even as divorce attorneys are alert to such dealings, divorce judges seem less inclined to cooperate with such obvious imbalances in a financial plan.

Today's Divorcing Generation May Include Your Kids.

While the Family Partnership may have been somewhat curtailed in the courtroom with regard to spousal inequity, this type of planning does work very handily for ensuring that gifts of Partnership interests made to children stay in the family in the event of divorce. This is good news for the family in view of the fact that today's 30- and 40-year-olds are more prone to divorce than any generation that preceded them.

Let's first look at the conventional estate plan in which there is little to protect children from the consequences of learning experiences such as divorce. If, for example, they received an outright gift of cash or securities, such assets are frequently intermingled with the receiving couple's other funds. Perhaps these moneys are used to make a down payment on a house, buy a car or pay off debts. Overall, when assets are gifted in this way, a number of unpleasant situations may result:

1) Frequently such gifts are not invested as wisely as when the parents had control.

2) Most often, the money simply gets spent.

3) If not spent, the money might become joint property subject to the claim of equal ownership in the case of a divorce.

Assuming the funds or assets survive being spent, but end up becoming joint property, such property will most probably be divided between the child and his or her spouse in the event of divorced. There are other risks such as failed business, bankruptcy, lawsuits or foreclosure, any of which could result in one's precious income, assets and saved estate tax being, ultimately, lost.

For example, instead of giving your son $10,000 outright each year, let's see how using a Family Partnership could prevent the negative outcomes we have just discussed. Assuming that the Partnership is set up with annual transfers to the son of $10,000 in Family Partnership interests, the income taxes on the money that the $10,000 earns are now in the son's lower tax bracket and the $10,000 and its subsequent growth are out of the parents' taxable estate. Immediately, a couple of improvements result:

1) The money is at no risk of being spent, consumed, or invested unwisely by the son.

2) The money cannot be co-mingled with the couple's other money because it is not in the form of cash.

Next, suppose the son and his wife wanted to buy a house or start a business and need a down payment or investment capital. The Partnership with the parents at the helm could loan the son, or the couple, the money for a home mortgage, a business, even a car. And, if they get a divorce or experience a business setback, they would still owe the Partnership the money regardless of who ended up with the business or property. Should the parents later desire to do so, however, they could change tactics and distribute funds to the son by redeeming the interests into cash.

In Summary.

A Family Partnership can effectively prevent funds that have been gifted from being lost to the estate in the event of an offspring's divorce or business failure. Additionally, if a Family Partnership is used to gift the beneficiaries interest instead of cash, control of the estate and its investments are maintained and money can be loaned - at interest to the Partnership - for genuine investment purposes. Additionally, principal via a distribution or redemption can be gifted if so desired at a later date.

CHAPTER
9

Being Elderly Doesn't Mean
Being Out of Control.

In order to eliminate estate tax, most plans recommend that the parents transfer control of their assets or money from themselves to their children or some other person who will act as trustee for their children. While in some instances this is necessary, generally speaking, it is a plan to be avoided. Rather, it seems a better option to keep the control of money or assets in the hands of those who earned or own it, so that the estate can continue to grow larger as, with proper planning, the taxes grow smaller. While the purpose of the preceding chapters has been to offer strategies that that will accomplish these goals, we would now like to address the General Partners who are no longer active in the business world and who wish to relax.

Frequently at this point in the estate planning process, the children may be in higher tax brackets than the parents and the parents are ready to increase their cash flow from the

Partnership in order to more fully enjoy life. This discussion will focus on how a Family Partnership helps with this type of planning, but first we're going to take a brief look at what the options would be under the "typical" estate plan.

Estate Plan Style	How to Access Funds in Retirement
Direct gifts to children over life of cash, securities, etc.	Ask children for return of money, hope they have it and say yes.
Irrevocable trusts	Ask trustee for money. They must say no.

It is that simple to see that by putting others in charge of one's assets, a person loses control and becomes dependent on them for the return of any moneys when and if they are needed. It is also timely to remember here that the $10,000 per year gifts to children of present, or the $625,000 lifetime unified credit that might have been used to gain tax relief, are each irrevocable transactions meaning the parents cannot take those moneys back without serious tax consequence.

Given this background, let's study the ways in which a Family Partnership might increase income or cash flow in the latter years of life. Please note that each of these concepts should be studied separately, then applied in conjunction with current tax cases on the subject.

Ways to Increase General Partner Income From the Family Partnership.

1) As the General Partner is managing the Partnership's

investment and has been doing so for years, it's permissible for the General Partner to take a management fee in compensation for the work done to oversee the Partnership.

This fee could be anywhere from 1% annually of the Partnership's assets, if the portfolio is comprised of stocks and bonds, up to and including a percentage of the portfolio's profits. Many Partnerships include hedge funds which are really just actively managed investment pools which provide a percentage of profits for the managers. This type of compensation is especially suitable when the parents arrive at a lower income tax bracket than their children.

A caveat here: Any such income is going to be subject to payroll tax and may, if it is sizable, offset or reduce Social Security income. For some Partnerships and families, this may be a big concern.

2) An alternative is for the General Partner to borrow money from the Partnership and reinvest the money at a higher rate. This borrowing short and lending long would earn the parent an interest margin on the funds. If, in the process, the investment goes down to less than its cost, the parent would get a tax deduction on its sale which would further reduce estate taxes.

3) A third way to provide additional cash flow for the General Partner is to have the Partnership make a reverse mortgage of a certain sum per month for the rest of the General Partner's life. The reverse mortgage payment would be non-taxable to the General Partner and would not affect Social Security or its taxability but, rather, would accrue as a loan against the survivor's estate. At the death of the General Partner, the home or other identified property would belong to the Partnership in settlement of the debt and, when the loan is paid off, the accrued interest would be taxable income to the Partnership. This, however, may be acceptable as income taxes are lower than estate tax.

Such a transaction might even save more estate tax as the parent would be spending the principal to achieve that higher lifestyle. In fact, the U. S. Government is currently guaranteeing thousands of these type of loans made by banks and insurance companies through HUD.

4) Next, let's suppose the General Partner simply wants to take a fabulous cruise but doesn't want to use any of the remaining non-Partnership assets to finance such a trip. Correctly done, the General Partner could go into the Partnership and withdraw the funds as a loan, secured or unsecured. This loan could just accrue interest until the General Partner dies at which point it could be paid off with the remaining assets. Again in this scenario, the estate tax is lowered because the loan counts to reduce the estate and the General Partner achieves his or her purpose.

5) The General Partner can also get money from the Partnership in another creative fashion by making a distribution of Partnership principal, or cash to themselves to the extent of their remaining Limited Partnership interests, or by distributing to the children who then could make gifts of the money back to the parents.

This is a tremendous benefit over the conventional estate plan because the General Partner continues to maintain full control of where the money is and how it is invested. Having such future support funds available to the General Partner is also easier on the children as they won't have to worry about having to support their parents in their later years.

In Summary.

While in typical estate planning, the recommendation is that the aging parent relinquish control of the estate to the children or a selected trustee, the Family Partnership works to maintain control of the estate in the hands of the parent as General Partner giving him or her options for using those funds and flexibility in further investing while saving estate tax.

CHAPTER
10

A State in Point:
Florida's Intangible Tax.

F orward Note: This section is applicable only to those who are obligated to pay Florida intangibles tax which is approximately $2 per thousand of value.

In 1995, the Florida Department of Revenue issued several Technical Assistance Advisements (TAA's) which stipulated that intangible assets held by a foreign or non-Florida Partnership are exempt from the intangible tax, even if all the Partners are Florida residents. Further, any interest that Florida residents own in the Partnership is also exempt.

A case in point comes from Philip Frost, a highly successful dermatologist from Miami, Florida, who bought a small pharmaceutical company called Key Pharmaceuticals for $100,000 then sold it to Schering Plough for hundreds of millions of dollars.

On March 16, 1987, Philip Frost filed a Certificate of Limited Partnership with the State of Nevada for a new Partnership called Frost Nevada Limited Partnership. As noted from the scant information which is required for filing in Nevada, the General Partner of Frost Nevada Limited is a corporation called Frost Nevada Corporation and, as he has no children, Philip is its only Limited Partner. As Limited Partner, Philip contributed to the Partnership $107,000,000 in fair value marketable securities.

The apparent reason for Dr. Frost's filing in Nevada was for the purpose of saving the intangible tax on the $107,000,000 Partnership which would have amounted to $214,000 per year. While it took over seven years for the State of Florida to agree with Dr. Frost's apparent motive and interpretation of the law, the case was finally approved and it is legal and acceptable to avoid intangible tax in this manner.

The state of Florida is not pleased with the trend of the state's wealthiest people avoiding intangible tax. So make hay while the sun shines!

CHAPTER
11

Monetary Miscellany.

T hus far we have seen how the Family Partnership can be an asset to billionaires, small business owners, doctors, and professionals who are concerned with liabilities, as well as people who are getting ready for Medicaid planning. Family Partnerships can also protect assets in the case of Limited Partners who are underage, going through divorces, or having business problems. Overall, the Partnership works for people with big families or people with small families who have investments that are appreciating.

In this chapter the discussion will focus on add-ons to the basic Family Partnership, these are fast track bells-and-whistles some of which are for special use only. Additionally, we are not necessarily recommending any of the ideas herein mentioned as many of them have not been as well tested as others. Therefore, this chapter is offered merely as financial food for thought.

Layers of Partnerships Upon Partnerships

As we have already learned under which certain circumstances, the IRS, courts and the stock market allow for the taking of discounts on the value of Limited Partnership interests. Based on this fact, and although untested in the courts, the next concept for discussion is, if the IRS through proper appraisal allows a Family Partnership to be discounted for valuation purposes, then why multi-layer them for greater savings?

Examples

If the Limited Partnership interests of Limited Partnership A are worth 70% of their nominal value and these are then contributed to Partnership B, would those interests be further discounted by another 30% and, if so, are further discounts possible until substantially all of the taxable value has been reduced? In theory, the answer is yes.

Would someone pay less for a Limited Partnership interest that would only hold Limited Partnerships interests than they would for a Limited Partnership that owned real property? Yes, we think they would. Further, in such a design, we think the following is of special importance:

Each layer of the Partnership must exist for a business reason, therefore, simply duplicating the documents in not nearly enough. However, having non-family members placed strategically in the design might be a help in achieving limitless savings as well as having different General Partners. We add a note of caution here as this design is not for the faint of heart but, if boldly and legally used, might save untold millions for the person courageous enough to test it.

Offshore Trusts as Limited Partners.

Offshore trusts are very interesting and, if properly set up, can be very successful in providing creditor protection. However, for the law-abiding U. S. person, offshore trusts provide only limited income tax benefits. This is due to the fact that a U.S. citizen is required to pay income tax on world-wide sources of income, meaning that simply having a trust in the Cayman Islands does not alleviate one of the responsibility of paying income taxes.

While the use of offshore trusts has proven to be a good creditor protection strategy, the near-exclusive use of such does conger up the thought and intention of fraudulent conveyance which might be something to be avoided. However, by adhering to the provision of a Limited Partnership of withholding 20% income tax on any amount due non-U.S. persons, one might achieve some further legal relief. Note: It is still unclear at this writing if a foreign trust can be deemed a grantor trust under U.S. law which would exempt it from this withholding.

In using such trusts and making gifts, the Crummey case and the tax law that it invoked are other concerns that must be taken into account. Remember that in order for a gift to qualify as a gift of a present interest, the gift must not be made in trust or, if it is made in trust, the trust must also contain the Crummey provisions of notice of the gift and the right to withdraw same. The gift must also be included in the beneficiaries estate if the beneficiary dies before the trust terminates. This Crummey provision is what makes a gift of insurance premiums into a trust gift of present interest. See Chapter 5.

Additionally, the Crummey provisions require that notice of any transfer made into the trust as a gift for a beneficiary must be set up to allow the benefactor within a certain specified period of time each year to inform the beneficiary of the gift and allow the beneficiary the right to withdraw the gift.

However, the question of whether or not a foreign trust can also be a Crummey trust remains. This strategy is quite technical in nature and subject to modification as the courts study and rule on these various points. Presently, we have found only rare uses for having foreign trusts be Partners due to these complexities combined with our understanding of various other less aggressive ways to obtain much the same benefit.

The Defective Trust

The defective trust is a special trust which recognizes that a gift has been made for transfer tax - estate and gift - purposes but doesn't recognize that it has been made for income tax purposes. Basically, the principal is given to the beneficiaries, but tax is still to be paid by the person gifting on the income that it generates. This can be a very effective tool in a couple of situations.

The first use for the defective trust is when the General Partner is in a much lower income tax bracket than the children, the Limited Partners. Here the General Partner wants the principal moved over to the children's estates, but wants to be taxed at in the lower bracket. Properly set up, the trust of which the children are beneficiaries, gets to keep the cash and the parents get to pay the tax from other funds.

This concept is different than the charging order that was discussed in Chapter 6, as the charging order separates the ownership and responsibility of paying the income tax while it is in place. A defective trust does this same thing more or less permanently.

Another situation where the defective trust may be helpful is when there is a very large estate or an urgent situation where there are only a few years to lower the taxable estate. In this case, taxable investment cash can be moved into a defective trust which would then hold the Limited Partnership units and the person who gave them away - not necessarily but usually the General Partner - would be responsible for paying the taxes on them.

For example, let's look at a $10,000,000 estate comprised primarily of real estate earning $1,000,000 per year. The owner could set up a Limited Partnership and contribute the property to the Partnership. Then the Partner makes large discounted gifts of Limited Partnership interests to a defective trust, the beneficiaries of which are his heirs. They would thus, considering the discounts, receive some $1,000,000 worth of property in the trust.

The defective trust would receive the K-1 from the Partnership representing a 10% of the total income as the trust owns 10% of the total ($1,000,000/$10,000,000). The trust would keep the income that was paid out in cash, if any, but the taxability of that income would go back to the person who set up the trust.

In short, the parents would have to pay the income taxes on money or equity that the trust retains for its beneficiaries. Assuming the income tax rate is 40%, then our former owner of the property would have to pay $40,000 out of his pocket in taxes. This further saves $20,000 in estate taxes because his estate is $40,000 smaller.

In general, however, we don't use these types of solutions for long-term situations as the rules regarding them are subject to modification and the trusts tend to be difficult and expensive to change.

Advanced Planning Pointer # 10
Defective Trusts.

The big question with defective trusts is who owns the basis of the taxes that were paid. This is an advanced strategy that should only be employed upon adequate advice and counsel from someone who understands the intricacies involved.

Irrevocable Trusts as Partners.

Like the offshore trusts, irrevocable trusts can be Partners of Family Limited Partnerships. The issues we often face with this scenario is that the irrevocable trust is irrevocable (loss of control) and it has a compressed income tax bracket. Hence, it reaches its maximum income tax bracket at about $7,500 in taxable income per year. So, if this Partnership is intended to generate taxable income it might be advisable to use some other vehicle to be the Limited Partner.

Another issue comes up as well. The Limited Partnership has the relatively unique feature - actually unique to Partnership S corporations and limited liability companies - of being able to pass out income without having to hand out the cash that goes with it. This a very handy feature. However, when we combine it with an irrevocable trust with its compressed tax rates, it may backfire.

Suppose the Partnership makes $25,000 for the Limited Partner which is an irrevocable trust also called a complex trust. Then the General Partner decides not to distribute the income. This means that the trust as a Limited Partner will have to pay income tax on the $25,000 at the 40% rate. This could be avoided if the Partnership actually distributes the $25,000 in cash and then the trust - providing its terms allow - distributes the funds to the trust beneficiaries. Even if all this happens, the money ended up distributed to the kids anyway, and other than having earned discounts and having a little more choice, nothing much has been accomplished.

When set up in a proper, timely fashion, irrevocable trusts can generally be well-used as creditor avoidance vehicles.

CHAPTER
12

The Promise of the Family
Limited Partnership.

As this book has primarily been devoted to detailing the limitless benefits and flexibility of the Family Limited Partnership, it seemed that it would be helpful to provide an encapsulation of the estimated costs and potential savings of this powerful financial vehicle. Therefore, outlined in this chapter are some typical costs and anticipated savings that result from the setup of a Family Partnership.

Estimating Potential Annual Tax Savings Using the Family Partnership.

NOTE: To help illustrate this concept please refer to Chart A.

A-1) Begin by entering the marginal tax bracket, generally from 28% to 39.6%.

A-2) Estimate the income tax brackets of all Limited Partners. The bracket for minors is generally 0% to 15%. Each child under the age of 14 gets the first $1,300 in investment income tax free, then they are in their parent's tax bracket until their age 14. At age 14, they assume their own bracket.

A-3)   Determine the difference between income tax brackets.

A-4)   Calculate the amount of taxable income which will be shifted into the Partnership by multiplying the total investment income of the Partnership times the percentage that will be transferred away in year one.

A-5)   The resulting figure is the annual income tax saving of the Partnership.

NOTE: Include state or local income taxes where applicable.

CHART A - ANNUAL INCOME TAX SAVINGS.

	Example	Yours
1) Tax Bracket of Creators	39.60%	_____
2) Average Tax Bracket of Limited Partners	15.00%	_____
3) Difference between Brackets	24.60%	_____
4) Taxable Income to be Shifted	$30,000	_____
5) Income Tax Savings (annually and increasing)	**$ 7,380**	_____

Estimating Potential Annual Estate Tax Savings Using a Family Partnership.

NOTE: To help illustrate this concept please refer to Chart B.

B-1)   Add up the number of heirs to receive transfers.

B-2)   Add in the amount of interest they are to receive.

B-3)   Multiply B-2 by B-1 to get the total annual transfer.

B-4)   Multiply the estate tax rate of 50% by B-3. In our example, that would be $100,000 X 50.00%.

B-5)   The result of B-4 would be your estimated annual tax savings. Over time, this figure will increase due to the interest earned or the growth of the assets.

CHART B - ANNUAL ESTATE TAX SAVINGS.

	Example	Yours
1) Number of Heirs to Receive Interests	5	_____
2) Amount of Interest to be Received	$20,000	_____
3) Total Annual Transfers (B-1 x B-3)	$100,000	_____
4) Estate Tax Rate	50.00%	_____
5) Estimated Estate Tax Saved (Annually)	**$50,000**	_____

The estate tax calculation assumes that the estate tax savings is based upon the amount of transfers and ignores the use of discounts and appreciation of the underlying property.

Estimating Consumption Tax Savings Using the Family Partnership.

NOTE: To help illustrate this concept please refer to Chart C.

C-1) Enter the total amount of transfers that will be made under the Limited Partnership arrangement, typically $10,000 per parent per child, assuming a consumption tax rate of 100%. Consumption tax is that loss which might occur when you give money to heirs and they spend it.

CHART C - ANNUAL CONSUMPTION "TAX" SAVINGS.

	Example	Yours
1) Enter the Amount of Annual Transfers	$100,000	_____
2) Less: Estate Tax saved from Chart B	$50,000	_____
3) Amount Subject to Consumption "Tax"	$50,000	_____
4) Tax Rate	50%	_____
5) Consumption Tax Saved	**$25,000**	_____

Additional Savings Using a Family Partnership.

Chart D illustrates additional annual tax savings available. For example:

D-1) Florida residents should add the amount of intangible tax saved.

D-2) If the creditor advantages of this Partnership have any value, the dollar value should be affixed.

D-3) Savings associated with any discounts that can be taken should then be figured in.

CHART D - OTHER ANNUAL SAVINGS AND ECONOMIES.

	Example	Yours
1) Intangible Tax Savings	2,000	_____
2) Value of Assets being more protected from creditors	2,000	_____
3) Valuation Discounts on Annual Gifts (typically 30% of gift x estate tax rate)	10,000	_____
4) Value of Control of Assets	10,000	_____
5) Value of QDOT features	20,000	_____
6) Value of Protecting Heirs Inheritances from Divorces	10,000	_____
7) Value of Managing Larger Sums of Money: Unit vs. Small Accounts	5,000	_____
8) Other Values	—	_____

Other Savings and Economies Total $59,000 _____

CHART E - SUMMARY OF ANNUAL TAX SAVINGS.

	Example	Yours
A-5) Income Tax Savings (annually increasing)	$7,380	_____
B-5) Estimated Estate Tax Saved (annually)	$50,000	_____
C-5) Consumption Tax Saved	$25,000	_____
D-9) Other savings -economics	$59,000	_____
Total Estimated Annual Savings	**$141,380**	_____

One-Time Estate Tax Savings

The value here is in the transfer of the appreciation of the Unified Credit to the heirs.

NOTE: To help illustrate the one-time estate tax savings please refer to Chart F.

F-1)   The amount of unified credit to be used (maximum is $1,250,000).

F-2)   Estimate on what the unified credit (F-1) would be worth upon the second death.

F-3) The difference in the appreciation (F-2 minus F-1).

F-4) The estate tax saved by making transfers. This calculation is 50% of the difference in appreciation (F-3).

F-5) Add in the estate tax savings incurred due to discounts allowed in a Family Limited Partnership transfer. (F-1 x the estate tax rate of 50.00% x 30.00% discount.)

CHART F - ONE-TIME ESTATE TAX SAVINGS.

		Example	Yours
F-1)	Amount of Unified Credit to be used	$650,000	_____
F-2)	Estimated Worth at Second Death	$2,000,000	_____
F-3)	Difference	$1,400,000	_____
F-4)	Estate Tax Saved	$700,000	_____
F-5)	Savings in Estate Tax due to Discounts	$90,000	_____
Total One-Time Estate Tax Savings		**$790,000**	_____

When figures for the total annual savings and the one-time estate tax savings are significant, a Family Partnership would more than likely be advantageous.

Costs Associated with Operation of Family Partnerships.

Here are some of the approximate startup costs of a Partnership NOTE: To help illustrate these costs please refer to Chart G.

G-1) State filing fee is usually a nominal sum of approximately $250. (While there is no requirement to file in Florida, the maximum fee is $1800.)

G-2) Registered agent fee for out-of-state Partnerships.

G-3) Legal and consulting fee is dependent on the complexity of and time involvement in the Partnership.

G-4) The cost involved in re-titling assets and documentary stamps into the Partnership.

G-5) Appraisal fees of the Partnership interests - optional to earn discounts.

G-6) Express mail and miscellaneous fees.

G-7) Setup accounting fees.

CHART G - STARTUP COSTS.

		Example	Yours
G-1)	State Filing Fees	$ 250.	_____
G-2)	Registered Agent Fee	$ 150.	_____
G-3)	Legal and Consulting Fee	$ 9,500.	_____
G-4)	Re-title Assets/ Doc. Stamp Costs	$ 500.	_____
G-5)	Appraisal Fees	$ 3,000	_____
G-6)	Express Mail & Misc. Fees	$ 250.	_____
G-7)	Setup Accounting Fees	$ 400.	_____
Total Setup Costs		**$14,050**	_____

Annual Costs Associated with
Family Limited Partnerships.

NOTE: To help illustrate these costs please refer to Chart H.

H-1) Annual state registration fees range from $75 to highest fees of, approximately, $600 for Florida Partnerships.

H-2) Annual registered agent fees, if applicable.

H-3) Annual cost of accountant depending on the complexity of the books.

H-4) Appraisal fee (occasional, if required).

H-5) Any other possible costs, such as legal fees.

CHART H- ANNUAL COSTS.

		Example	Yours
H-1)	Annual State Fees	$200.	_____
H-2)	Annual Registered Agent Fees	150.	_____
H-3)	Accounting	650.	_____
H-4)	Appraisal Fees (occasional)	400.	_____
H-5)	Other (legal fees)	Varies	_____
	Total Annual Costs	**$1,400.**	_____

NOTE: these annual expenses are generally deductible.

COMPARISON OF BENEFITS VS. COSTS.

	Example	Yours
ANNUAL		
Benefits (Savings)	$95,220	_____
Costs	$1,400	_____
ONE TIME		
Benefits (Savings)	$790,000	_____
Setup Costs	$14,050	_____

CHAPTER
13

Questions and Answers

1. How is a Family Partnership set up?

Prepared by an attorney, the Family Partnership is a written agreement which designates control and direction of assets and is signed by all family members who are to be included in the Partnership. After the legal document has been signed, assets must be transferred into the Partnership.

Typically, once the Partnership has been signed and funded, the creators transfer some of their Limited Partnership interests to children or other family members. This is usually accomplished through a simple memo sent to the attorney or an accountant. Additionally, if the Partnership initially includes only linear descendants, other family members such as spouses may be added as Partners at a later time.

2. Does a Partnership agreement become public record?

The Partnership agreement is not public record. However, under each state law, a Partnership certificate is registered with the Division of Corporations. Depending on the state laws governing a specific agreement, this certificate generally reflects the names of the General Partners and does not detail the names of the Limited Partners. The agreement containing the terms for the operation of the Family Partnership by the General Partners does not become public record and remains private.

3. Which states provide for Family Partnerships?

All states but Louisiana have adopted the Revised Uniform Limited Partnership Act. Except for filing fees, which vary from state to state, the laws of each state are fairly consistent concerning the operation of the Family Partnership, through there are differences between Louisiana Limited Partnership Law and the Uniform Act. As with any business, the Internal Revenue Code governs the taxability regarding the profits and losses of the Partnership. (Other pertinent Louisiana issues covered in questions 37, 38 and 39.)

4. How much does a Family Partnership cost to set up and operate?

See Chapter 12 for a complete discussion of the estimate costs and benefits.

5. Does a Family Partnership require the filing of an income tax return and payment of taxes?

The Family Partnership is treated as a business under the Internal Revenue Code which means that an annual Partnership income tax return must be filed by the General

Partner. However, this return is used for informational purposes only. The Partnership does not pay income tax on any profits it earns annually, nor is it allowed to take a deduction for any losses it incurs. Just as with an S corporation, the Family Partnership is a pass-through entity as far as income taxes are concerned. Partners must report on their annual income tax return their share of Partnership profits and expenses. However, one of the most attractive aspects of the Family Partnership is that it provides for the use of the lower tax brackets of the Partners' children to offset these income figures.

6. How much can be saved with a Family Partnership?

See Chapter 12 for an extensive discussion regarding the potential benefits of a Family Partnership.

7. Who controls the operation of the Family Partnership and to what extent?

The General Partner controls the operation of the Family Partnership as, by law, the Limited Partners are not allowed to participate in the decision making or control of the Partnership. When a Partnership is created, a General Partner or Partners are designated. The ability of the General Partner to control the Partnership is of paramount importance as the General Partner decides what money or assets can come into the Partnership, how to value any additions, whether they will be sold, traded or leveraged and at what terms and prices. The General Partner also gets to determine what distributions are to be made from the Partnership. Therefore, it is vitally important to the well-being of the Partnership that the General Partner, in carrying out the fiduciary responsibilities of the agreement, be reasonable, agreeable and in accord with the other members of the Partnership.

8. What happens if a Partner dies?

Typically, the will of the Partner will dictate who inherits his or her Partnership interest. If a General Partner dies and there are no remaining General Partners, the Partnership law provides for the termination of the agreement unless the remaining Limited Partners agree, within a certain number of days, to elect a new General Partner and continue the Partnership.

In many cases, the General Partner's interest will be held by a trust which will, in the event of the death, incapacity or bankruptcy of the General Partner, allow the Partnership to continue. The General Partner, in setting up that trust, would determine who replaces him or her and such designations may be changed as often as the General Partner chooses. If it is a Limited Partner who dies, then his or her interests will be handled in accordance with their wills or trusts.

9. Can a Family Partnership be set up so that even if a death occurs, the Partnership is guaranteed to continue?

A Partnership can be safeguarded against termination in the event of the death of the General Partner. The law that provides for the termination on the death of the only surviving General Partner unless the remaining Limited Partners continue the Partnership also mandates dissolving the Partnership in the event of the incompetence or bankruptcy of the last remaining General Partner. This can be overcome by establishing the Partnership with the General Partner as a trustee, corporation, or LLC. In the case of a trustee, if a Partner becomes incompetent or dies, the successor trustee named in advance becomes the new General Partner. In this way, one can insure against the Partnership being dissolved in the event of death or incompetence. This also allows the advantage of naming a series of successor trustees to be General Partner and the flexibility of changing trustees as circumstances dictate.

10. While I expect my assets to grow and increase in value, do I have to distribute the profits or income the Partnership makes each year?

As General Partner, you decide whether or not to distribute the earnings or principal to the Partners. This decision is entirely up to the General Partner to make unless the agreement that you have drafted states otherwise. The Partnership agreement can be written to provide for the yearly or more frequent distribution of earnings to the Partners. However, most parents establishing a Family Partnership wish to make this decision from year to year. Therefore, structuring the agreement so that the General Partner decides when and to what extent distributions are made is the most common form when the parent decides to control this factor. However, in the event that the General Partner decides to distribute the net earnings of the Partnership, the distribution must be made to all Partners in the proportion to each Partner's interest in the Partnership.

11. How do I put property into the Partnership and what do I receive back for my contributions?

You put property into a Partnership by contributing it. In exchange for the value of your contribution, you receive Partnership interests. Your property is valued at the date of the contribution based on its net fair market value. For example, if you contributed a $100,000 stock portfolio and a $200,000 piece of real estate which is subject to a $100,000 mortgage, your net contribution would be $200,000. In the typical estate planning and establishment of a Family Partnership, you, as a General Partner, would receive a 1% interest as a General Partner and 99% as a Limited Partner based on the value of your contribution. Your General Partner interest would thus be worth and valued at $2,000 or 1% of the Partnership value and your limited Partnership interest would be $198,000 or 99% of the total Partnership value. Note: These are the nominal values. The IRS and the tax court provide a basis for a lesser valuation based on a discount. See Advanced Planning Pointer #2 in Chapter 2.

12. Can I and other members of my family contribute additional property to the Family Partnership over and above what I contributed when I established it?

Yes. You and other family members as Partners can contribute more property to the Partnership after it is established should the agreement provide for it. The typical agreement requires the consent of the General Partner for the contribution of additional property. Naturally, the contribution of additional property will change the percent of each Partner's interest in the Partnership even though the nominal value of the non-contributing Partner will be unchanged.

13. Do I have to make gifts or transfer Partnership interest to my children?

No. Gifts of Partnership interest are made by transferring a percentage of the Limited Partnership interests you own to your children and, typically, following a strategy of planned giving whereby you annually transfer a percentage interest equal to $10,000 to each child. A married couple can transfer $20,000 in value to each Limited Partner. Gifts of Partnership interest are not required to be made by you. However, gifts of Partnership interest would call into play that most valuable aspect of the Partnership, which is to reduce the size of the estate that is subject to the tax by removing the future appreciation from your estate even as you retain control of all assets.

14. Does the Family Partnership have a name?

Yes. Just like a corporation, a Family Partnership must have a name. Many people prefer to use their family name while others prefer to use a name not related to their family. Others use the Partnership name to honor a parent or loved one. Some states require that the words "Limited Partnership" be used in the name while other states require the abbreviation LP. Examples follow: The Smith Family Limited Partnership; Medical Leasing Partners LP: the ABC Partnership. Customarily, the Partnership attorney determines through the state's Division of Corporations and Partnerships the name's availability prior to filing the Certificate of Limited Partnership.

15. Are there any tax law cases on Family Partnerships and valuation discounts on gifting of Partnership interests as well as discounts on death of a Partner?

Yes. There are many tax law cases which discuss Family Partnerships using discounts on gifting of Partnership interests and discounts on the value of Partnership interest on the death of a Partner. While the facilitating attorney should be able to obtain information on the most current cases and details, it should be noted that the IRS does not allow for the over use of discounts. The figures used in this book are conservative and realistic in today's environment. A tax advisor can provide an update on what the trend is when a Partnership is being set up and further advise you on how to arrive at discount values through the use of appraisals and other means acceptable to the IRS.

16. Is a Family Partnership suitable for Medicaid planning?

Yes. See Chapter 6 for a full discussion.

17. Should I put all my property and money into the Partnership?

Whether or not you put all of you money or property into a Partnership is an issue that should be discussed with your attorney and financial advisor. Generally, the recommendation would be to not put all property and money in a Family Partnership. One's residence, for example, is not generally considered as having a business purpose so, typically, it would not be included in the Partnership which would leave any income from that property free for individual use. While there is presently a bill in front of Congress that will so allow, under current law an S Corporation cannot contribute stock and keep the election. IRAs, qualified funds and certain annuities can not generally be contributed.

18. How does it happen that a General Partnership can have all control with the Limited Partners having no rights to control.

The law and the agreement among the Partners provide the General Partner with the authority to operate the Family Partnership and, therefore, make all the decisions for the Partnership's business and investments as to what is bought and sold, whether or not to make distributions of the Partnership's earnings and to what extent. Limited Partners, consequently, are prohibited by law from operating the Partnership or interfering in the decisions made by the General Partner or Partners. Consequently, the law provides that the General Partners are liable for any debts or obligations of the Partnership to the extent that the Partnership's assets are insufficient to pay these obligations. Whereas a General Partner is individually liable for any such debts of the Partnership, a Limited Partner has no individual liability for satisfying debts of the Partnership where there are insufficient assets to pay these debts.

The justification for this is found in the fact that it is the General Partner who makes the decisions as to the business of the Partnership and, to the extent that their decisions were bad decisions resulting in the Partnership incurring debts without property or assets to satisfy those debts, the General Partner should be held accountable for such debts.

The use of Family Partnerships for estate and tax planning as we have herein discussed is quite different than the use of Family Partnerships to operate on-going businesses with employees where liability and risk are a daily concern. Such operating businesses require quite different entities such as corporations that provide the corporation owners with protection from liability which might result from insufficient assets of the corporation to pay its debts.

19. How fast and how often can I transfer Partnership interests to my children or other persons?

In order to answer this question, a review of the tax law concerning gifts is required. The tax law allows each person to transfer property valued up to $10,000 per calendar year without paying a gift tax or filing a gift tax return. The gifts of Limited Partnership interests made to children each year can be equal to $10,000 per child. In addition, discounts are allowed on the value of the Partnership interest, thereby allowing more than $10,000 in nominal value of Partnership interest to be transferred annually. In the case that the Partnership agreement contains certain limitations and a proper appraisal of the Partnership interest is made which establishes any such discounts, an amount greater than the $10,000 annual gift is allowed. The Harrison case referenced in Question #33 provides the classic example for utilizing maximum gifts and discounts to accomplish, in a relatively short period of time, maximum tax savings. Finally, in the case where a spouse is not a U.S. citizen, different rules apply as to the value of outright gifts or Partnership interest one is allowed to give.

20. What is a form K-1?

A form K-1 is provided when the Partnership's annual income tax is prepared. As the Partnership pays no income taxes, the net profit or loss is determined through a form K-1 which is prepared to show each Partner's loss or profit based on that Partner's percentage of ownership in the Partnership. The information on the K-1 is included in each Partner's annual income tax return. Each Partner then pays income tax on the additional income reflected on the K-1.

21. Once a gift of Limited Partnership interest is made, can the recipient redeem, sell or transfer his or her interest?

Some states allow a Partner to redeem his or her interest, providing the Partnership with at least six months to redeem such interest. If it is the parents who are establishing a Partnership, it is usually the recommendation that they choose to register their Partnership in a state that does not allow for such redemption.

Further, any transfer, in order to be legally considered a gift, must be a transfer of a present interest. As such, the interest in the Partnership can be transferred to others by your child, however, the limitations on the transferability are normally provided through provisions in the Partnership agreement when it is created. These provisions are normally similar to those in a family corporation prohibiting transfer of Partnership interest by a child unless the Partnership is first offered the opportunity to purchase said interest. In this regard, the decision as to whether or not the Partnership will purchase said interest is determined by the General Partner.

In other words, in accordance with tax law, interests that are transferred to your children must be further transferable by them to others. However, reasonable restrictions can be put into place that will most probably and effectively keep those interests in the family.

22. Is all this Partnership business too complicated to be worthwhile?

Many people in the first few months of setting up their first corporation or business find it complicated to deal with the accounting and tax forms. As with many other things, after the initial startup, the dealings become more familiar, the mechanics and operational things falling right into place. At this point, most people wish they had turned to the Partnership earlier, for all its benefits.

23. Is it only children who can become Limited Partners or can nephews, nieces, cousins, friends, even charitable organizations be included in the agreement?

Any heir, relative or person of choice can be gifted an interest and, thus, become a Limited Partner in a Family Limited Partnership. Generally, Partners are kept to U.S. residents, trusts, corporations or other Partnerships. The recipient must accept the interest and agree to the Partners' terms.

24. Can a General Partner receive money for services as General Partner?

Yes. The Partnership agreement can provide that the General Partner receive a reasonable compensation for his or her services as General Partner. The Partnership can also provide that the compensation be deferred with any such moneys coming into the General Partner or Partners being taken at some future date when and if desired by the General Partner.

25. When the Partnership's assets increase in value, do the contributing Partner and General Partner get to keep the increased value?

Once a contribution of property has been made to the Partnership, any increase in value to the Partnership property is part of the Partnership and, to the extent that it is not distributed, each Partner owns the percentage of the value of the Partnership equal to the increase in the asset's value. Further, to the extent that a distribution of Partnership income or Partnership property is made, each Partner receives the value or the distribution based on his or her percentage of ownership as a Partner. For a more in-depth discussion, see Chapter 1.

26. What advantage would a Family Partnership have over a living trust?

Both the living trust and the Family Partnership can be used to avoid the necessity of appointing a guardian of property if incompetence occurs and probate administration in the event of death. However, a living trust does not provide an insulation of assets from creditors or a discount for federal estate tax evaluation purposes and does not allow a person to make gifts of property while remaining in control of his or her own property. Additionally, if a living trust were to remain in existence after one's death, so as to allow for growth of the estate for the longer term benefit of the children, the trust might well incur higher taxes and suffer adverse tax consequences which would be avoided through the use of a Family Partnership. Those people who grasp the benefits and flexibility of the Family Partnership report that they highly prefer it over living trusts, irrevocable trusts, or life insurance trusts to reduce or eliminate federal estate tax. In many cases, it is used in conjunction with other powerful vehicles like the living trust, to get the best of all of them.

27. Can things go wrong when using the Family Partnership?

As with anything in life, if we do not get qualified help or advice in putting together a Family Partnership, defects can crop up. It is, therefore, imperative to seek the advice of competent, experienced financial people and attorneys to assist in creating a Partnership. Properly advised, one can for example, avoid being taxed as an association taxable as a corporation or sidestep any number of other pitfalls. All in all, it is imperative that your Family Partnership agreement be structured by someone who can ensure that it contains the provisions required to qualify as a bona fide Family Limited Partnership under applicable law.

28. If both the family attorney and accountant are unfamiliar with Family Limited Partnerships, how can one find competent help in this area?

Realizing that having trusted and competent advisors is vitally important to the accomplishment of all the recommendations that have been made with regard to the creation of effective Family Partnerships, we have provided a list in the Appendix 3 containing names and addresses of advisors who have expressed interest in assisting persons in accomplishing this level of planning.

29. Who is responsible for all the paper work that must be signed by the Partnership and do all the Partners have to sign if Partnership property is sold?

The General Partners are solely responsible for all of the management, buying and selling of any Partnership property. The General Partners can, therefore, among themselves delegate one Managing Partner whose signature is required anytime Partnership assets are sold or transferred.

30. What happens to a Limited Partner's interest in the case of divorce, bankruptcy, lawsuit or if the Partner becomes incompetent or dies.

We have discussed the ramifications of divorce on the Family Partnership in Chapter 4 and the impact of a lawsuit or bankruptcy on a Partnership in Chapter 6. As the Limited Partner has no management responsibilities, the matter of incompetence would have little if any effect on the Partnership. Further, when a Limited Partner dies, his or her interest is handled as his other assets. In other words, the beneficiary of the estate would inherit by operation of law whatever interest the decedent had. Note that, under current law, a valuation discount may be available to the estate.

31. What types of tax and regulation changes might occur which would affect a Family Limited Partnership?

While we have no way of predicting what types of tax and regulatory changes might face us in the future, to date experience has demonstrated that the safe and controlled transfer of assets between generations will never be easier or less expensive than through a Family Limited Partnership. Sam Walton was a good teacher. Please see Chapter 1.

32. Is it necessary for a Partnership to have a Corporate General Partner? Under what circumstances should a Corporate General Partner be used?

Taken together, the answer to these questions comes in two parts one from a business management/liability standpoint and the other from a tax viewpoint.

First, a Corporate General Partner is usually called for if the contents of the Partnership would tend to attract liabilities. For instance, a Partnership holding a stadium, coliseum, or place where the public gathers including office buildings would represent such a situation. In such cases, it is the job of the Corporate General Partner to effectively stop liabilities from "piercing the corporate veil" or landing on a Partner's personal balance sheet. Any personal action or negligence on behalf of the Partner would, of course, affect such protection that the General Partner could supply. Otherwise, in a Limited Partnership, the General Partner is responsible for the liabilities of the Partnership and for any excess liabilities the Partnership causes. If the General Partner happens to be a corporation, then that corporation should be liable to the extent that it has the assets to pay off the liabilities. Note that it is important for tax purposes that a Corporate General Partner have assets. However, even with severe liability, if the assets of the Corporate General Partner have become depleted, creditors have no place to go to because the shareholders of this type of corporation are not responsible for its debts. Therefore, the damage is mostly contained at that point.

In many cases, we have seen these types of liability producing assets being held in a person's name outright - e.g. Dr. Jones owns his office building in the name of Dr. Jones - placing the client at great risk. By placing that same property into a Family Limited Partnership, dramatic improvements are made in removing the client from exposure to possible catastrophic claims from creditors. This can be accomplished with a Corporate General Partner or without one by simply insulating this Partner's other assets from any excess liabilities from the office building.

The tax picture, however, is a little more intricate. In order for a Partnership to qualify as such for income tax purposes, it must not possess anymore than two of the four qualities the IRS attributes to an "association taxable as a corporation." These qualities include:

1) Unlimited life;

2) Centralization of management;

3) Limited liability;

4) Free transferability of interests.

Generally, the Partnership will possess two of these qualities.

The first; Centralization of management - Our General Partner runs the business; and the forth; Free transferability of interest - although we prefer to not have this characteristic, it is important that the interest be transferable in order to qualify as gifts of a present interest, hence, qualify for use of the annual $10,000 gift exclusion to give away interests.

If this is the case, it is critical that we do not possess the other two qualities: Item 1) unlimited life or Item 2) limited liability. With regard to unlimited life, please review the discussion under Question 33 regarding Code Section 2704. The limited liability question is the one applicable here.

If a Corporate General Partner has no equity or less than the arbitrary 10% number typically used, then it might be deemed to have the attribute of limited liability. Hence, under U.S. income tax law, the Partner could be deemed an "association taxable as a corporation." Should this occur, the Partnership itself might owe corporate tax, interest and penalties on all earned income from the applicable periods. Additionally, if any distributions were made, such distributions might be re-characterized as dividends which might change the tax picture of the Partners. It is, therefore, of primary importance that, if used, a Corporate General Partner be properly capitalized.

Additionally, in the case of a Corporate General Partner being held by another Partnership, most frequently a C corporation funded with tax exempt bonds or the like, these items must be calculated as to the cost of capital, operating costs, various tax brackets and so forth.

In short, the question of whether to use a Corporate

General Partner would be very easy to answer if there are high liability assets involved or very complicated depending on the Code Section 2704 implications. See Questions #33.

Further, recently the IRS has loosened these regulations to give us "check-in-the-box" authority to decide how an entity is to be taxed. This would seem to solve all the headaches brought on by the above discussion. Be careful, these regulations are not time-tested yet.

33. What does IRS Code Section 2704 have to do with Partnership design, term of life and discounts?

As this information is primarily included for the benefit of accountants and attorneys, the general reader may find it quite technical in nature. It should also be noted that obtaining valuation discounts is only one of the many reasons people form Family Limited Partnerships and may well represent an area of continuing modification by Congress and the IRS. Further, as with any technical area of the law, different advisors have different opinions. We, therefore, urge you to follow the opinion of your trusted advisor even if it should differ from the following.

IRS Code Section 2704 states that, if a lapse of a voting or liquidation occurs right at death with the immediate result that an individual or members of the family gain control of the entity, the lapsing of such right will not be considered in valuing or discounting property passing through the estate.

This code is based on the case of Estate of Daniel Harrison vs. Commissioner in which a Texas oilman transferred his oil and gas interests into a Limited Partnership along with the oil and gas interests of his two sons. The agreement provided that upon his death - which occurred <u>very</u>

shortly thereafter - his right to liquidate the Partnership held by his General Partner interest rather than by his Limited Partnership interest would receive his interest and could be purchased by his sons at face amount. Upon his death, his sons immediately re-purchased his General Partner interest at face value without the power to terminate the entire Partnership.

Under this agreement, the assets that passed through Mr. Harrison's estate simply became cash from the sale of the General Partner's interest and the Limited Partnership interest which represented the bulk of his holdings in the oil and gas Partnership. If, however, the estate had held onto the General Partner's interest, it could have redeemed those interests for full value by terminating the Partnership. Had this occurred, it would have required that the estate pay tax on the entire value rather than the lessor value represented by those interests being held in a non-redeemable Limited Partnership interests. In other words, as the estate did not have the power to redeem the Limited Partnership at full value, it was able to claim that the interest it owned was worth substantially less than its share of the whole because there was no power to liquidate. The result was that the estate claimed a massive discount, saving millions of dollars in estate tax.

In court, the estate won the case and Congress changed the law resulting in IRS Code Section 2704 which states that if a right - such as Mr. Harris's General Partnership interest right required the termination of a Partnership and the receipt of full value - lapses or terminates and, if that same right is held solely by other family members - then the passing of that right is considered a taxable gift.

Therefore, the value of that gift added to the discount value of the Limited Partnership interest which equaled the total value of the oil and gas properties and resulted in no benefit. Also see IRS Code Section 2704(a).

So, the Harrison design is no longer appropriate subsequent to the passage of IRS Code Section 2704. However, there are a number of other opportunities which still exist that could accomplish much the same result. Essentially, since the change of the law, we simply avoid providing lapsing interests to anyone, making the provisions generally inapplicable.

In another scenario, Mr. Harrison could have taken only Limited Partnership interests in exchange for his contribution to the Family Partnership rather than including the lapsing power or involving a non-family member in the Partnership. By choosing this option, Harrison's estate would still have gotten to take the valuation discounts under the new law as:

1) Involving a non-family member removes IRS Code Section from applicability. Note: Under Section 2704(c)(2), nieces or nephews are considered non-family members.

2) Should Harrison have had only Limited Partnership interests in his estate, there would have been no power to lapse, therefore, the gift or transfer value would have produced the same result.

While we believe that both of these provisions would still be viable today, this would not be a complete discussion without a discussion of applicable restrictions and those things which are considered exceptions to such applicable restrictions.

Applicable Restrictions under IRS Code Section 2704:

A restriction that effectively limits the ability of the entity to liquidate and (1) the restriction lapses in whole or part after the transfer or (2) the transferor or any member of his family, either alone or collectively, has the right to remove the restriction after the transfer.

Where the government gives us a definition it must also grant us exclusions to those definitions. The following are exclusions to applicable restrictions:

1) Such restrictions that prohibit termination or liquidation of the Partnership which are termed commercially reasonable and arise from any financing with an unrelated third party and,

2) Any restriction which is imposed or required to be imposed by any federal or state law.

The first exclusion is of little help, but the second can lead to the proper and legal taking of valuation discounts. On this subject, we will now answer a few more questions.

If, for example, a Partnership has only family members and has no other restrictions upon termination except a state required term limit - some states require that Partnerships renew themselves at a stipulated time - would this term limit be a restriction upon liquidation which lapses after a transfer?

We think not, as this restriction is imposed under state law and is, therefore, an exception to the applicable restriction definition referenced above.

However, some drafters of Limited Partnerships have chosen to register such agreements in states where the state allows unlimited lives. This action removes one question as it brings up another.

Usually the states that allow perpetual existence also allow the Limited Partners withdrawal rights. In this case, if there is no fixed date on which the Partnership terminates or is renewed, a remedy must be sought that will allow Partners to get their value out of the Partnership.

This is done by giving a time period - if not stated in the agreement this is usually six months by statute - for the Limited Partners to give notice to the Partnership of their intention to withdraw and their demand for fair value. If the document then, under the same state law, restricts the redemption on an per Partner basis to some time in the future, the exclusion would no longer be applicable as it is the document rather then the law which restricts the redemption of the interest thus earning the discount. Further, after the transfer is made, the document can be amended by the remaining 100% family members. The result is a clear applicable restriction as defined above.

These issues are not relevant to gifts made during life in accordance with IRS Code Section 2704, but, apply primarily to the discounts at death when it is the job of the plan to uncouple the interest of the General Partner decedent from the remaining Limited Partnership interest of the descendant in order to get discounts on the latter. In such cases, it is best to have a non-family member or entity as the General Partner which has some voting power over distributions and termination of the Partnership.

As these matters are quite technical, it is wisest in determining a course of action to work through competent counsel who is familiar with the applicable laws and arguments and will work to set up such an agreement in keeping with the amount of power that is being transferred away in order to earn future discounts.

34. What type of property can I transfer into a Limited Partnership?

Property typically contributed to a Family Limited Partnership consists of stock, bonds, securities, cash, mortgages and real property, other than one's residence. Certain other assets are not contributed either due to prohibitions in the law or adverse tax consequences to the contribution. These assets include, qualified funds; 401K moneys, IRA funds and certain annuities. When you contribute your property to the Family Partnership, the process is similar to funding a living trust. Where prior to contribution your name is reflected as owner of the property, after contribution, the Partnership's name is reflected as owner of the property.

Securities accounts currently in your name can be changed to the name of your Family Partnership. Any real estate transferred to the Partnership would require new deeds to be signed and recorded reflecting the transfer from you to the new Family Partnership. Any bank accounts, stock certificates or other assets would also be re-titled from your name to the name of the Family Partnership with yours and the other General Partners' names as General Partners.

See also discussion of special rules regarding contribution of negotiable securities in Advanced Planning Pointer # 3.

35. While putting S corporation stock into a Family Partnership causes the forfeiture of the S status of the corporation, what are the ramifications of contributing C stock and would that work?

While C stock can be contributed into a Family Partnership, it's important to note the effect of Code Section 2036(b). This Section of the Code states that - in the case of C stock being contributed to a Family Partnership with the Limited Partnership interests being given away, but the

General Partner maintaining voting control - the stock does not count as a gift.

While on the surface this isn't advantageous, it is possible to plan around this issue as follows:

1) Nominate a special General Partner - an unrelated person, CPA or attorney - who will be designated to vote only those shares which minimizes his or her impact on the overall Partnership.

2) Without transferring stock, transfer some of the earning power of the business into a Partnership through a properly structured lease or loan.

3) Determine the possibility of setting up a C corporation if one did not exist before the formation of the Family Partnership.

Again, the reminder in dealing with such technical matters is to have any such changes arranged or reviewed by competent counsel.

36. Suppose a Family Partnership is to be set up using the spouses $10,000 annual exclusions for each of 4 children and 7 grandchildren, or for 7 grandchildren born of only three of children. How can the use of annual exclusions be maximized to save taxes but keep the estate going equally to each of the four children and their children?

This can be done easily by using the maximum amount of the annual $10,000 gift exclusion which is computed by multiplying the number of grandchildren by $20,000 or $10,000 for each of two grandparents. Note: If the grandchildren are not gifted, the estate would be forfeiting the ability to make free gifts of $140,000 per year.

The initial loss of the use of the annual exclusions will increase the estate tax bill by $70,000 per year plus any growth on the money. However, this money can be recaptured and the estate gifts kept equal among the 4 children as follows:

The gifts of Limited Partnership interest are made to each child - perhaps including their spouses - as normal. Each grandchild also receives a full transfer of $20,000 in Limited Partnership interest. At this juncture, an inequity exists as the children who are parents are receiving more money through the gifts to their children than the childless offspring or couple.

In order to correct this inequity, the grandparents can contribute an equalizing amount of Partnership interests into a living trust for the benefit of the child who has no children. The transfer to this trust is not a gift, but does serve to hold that interest - plus growth - aside for the child who had been receiving less money as a result of being childless. When the grandparents have passed away, this special living trust would already have been designed to go solely and without tax to the designated child. Another separate living trust could be used for each child that had fewer than the highest number of children.

The net result is that each of the four children is treated equally, the estate tax is minimized and, in all probability, a good deal of income tax might also be saved due to the lower reporting income brackets of the grandchildren.

Alternately, should the unified credits not otherwise have been used, then we could force the gifts to be equal by using them to the extent it takes to equalize the four children.

37. Can personal savings type assets of Louisiana residents be held in a Nevada Family Limited Partnership and still receive all of the benefits of the Family Limited Partnership?

Yes. Personal savings assets of Louisiana residents can be held in Family Limited Partnerships of Nevada and other states and still receive the benefits of the use of Family Limited Partnerships. Income producing properties and business interests present a greater complication in this regard.

38. Can a Nevada Family Limited Partnership that holds income producing property and business interests of Louisiana residents be registered in the state of Louisiana?

Yes, the out of state partnership must register in Louisiana. A charging order under Nevada law probably won't apply to assets in Louisiana.

39. Can a Louisiana Limited Liability Company provide some of the same benefits that a Family Limited Partnership formed in other states provide?

Yes, a limited liability company formed in the state of Louisiana can provide a discounting, asset protection, income tax benefits, centralized control, etc. and, in fact may be more attractive in some ways than a limited partnership. Be sure to sued competent cousel, especially in this area.

APPENDIX

APPENDIX 1

Some Tax Aspects of Contributing Securities Portfolios to a Family Limited Partnership

The Investment Company Rules

The partnership format is ideal for contributing appreciated property, especially securities. The property passes into the partnership with no recognition of any unrealized gain or loss and the partnership takes over the cost basis of the contributing partner.

There are two little hoops that we have to jump through to make sure that this ability to contribute property without recognizing gain is not lost:

1) The partnership must operate like a business; and
2) The partnership must not provide "diversification".

As to the first item, which requires that the partnership operate like a business, is usually solved by establishing a "Statement of Business Purpose," which outlines the business goals of the partnership (growth, income preservation of principal, and so forth).

Whenever the partnership is almost entirely made up of securities and/or life insurance, we also like to suggest a professionally prepared "Investment Policy Statement" (IPS). An Investment Advisor, licensed and registered by either their respective state or the Securities and Exchange Commission usually prepares the IPS. For most of our partnerships, Stoll Financial Corp. prepares the IPS.

The second item, requires that the gains on securities which are contributed into the family partnership, be recognized if that contribution diversifies the contributor's portfolio. This is a relativity new law.

Years ago, wealthy industrialists used partnerships, such as the ones we set up, to mix and diversify their interests among themselves. This helped each of them diversify their own holdings by mixing them with the holdings or others, without capital gains tax.

Imagine, for example, that you are Bill Gates with a large position in one high growth company. Your portfolio changes in value by many millions of dollars a day. You would like to still have growth in your portfolio, but also have your portfolio be composed of many stocks instead of just one. You would also not want to pay the significant capital gains taxes that would be necessary for you to sell some of your stock and buy something else.

Imagine then that you are Ted Turner, the man who created CNN and has merged his empire into Time Life. You also have a lot of shares you would like to diversify and would like to do so without any capital gains taxes.

Likewise, with Michael Eisner of Disney, and many others, some not so famous, around the country.

The solution used to be, and thus the reason for the rule, that all these gentlemen would contribute some of their stock, (Gates would put in Microsoft, Turner some of his Time shares, Esiner some of his Disney and so forth), until the partnership had a more diversified portfolio. It made a lot of sense for people in that situation.

So the government changed the rules, this can no longer be done without paying tax on their capital gains.

Although the partnerships we set up are not intended to help the likes of Gates and Turner, we still must pay attention to the rules as I will describe herein, so we don't accidentally look like we are trying to get away with something.

The rules go like this,

TEST 1: If just one person, (person being a human being and/or their spouse), is the only contributor to a Limited Partnership then, even if they give away interests to their family, there is no diversification. That situation is the most common for us and so, the rule does not apply. If we pass this test, we need go no further. This area of the law does not keep someone from contributing a diversified portfolio to a Partnership, it only impedes those that try to gain diversification through a contribution to a Partnership.

TEST 2: This is the diversification test. If the transfer to the partnership results in diversification then we proceed to Test 3. But what is diversification? The Internal Revenue Code doesn't expressly say. The regulations in the code, however, does give us one example each of what does and what does not result in diversification.

The example describing what does not count as diversification, is basically a situation where one party contributes 100 shares of Stock A and another party contributes to the partnership 1 share of Stock B, (in theory the two stocks have similar market values). In such an example the regulations suggest that diversification does not exist. We call this a 1% test.

In the other example provided, they describe a situation where diversification does exist. It is equally of no help as it describes a situation where clearly a group of people are getting together to diversify their holdings as we described above in the hypothetical story regarding Gates and Turner.

If we feel that diversification has occurred in the creation or contribution to one of our partnerships, then we must go forward to Test 3.

TEST 3: This test is generally our "friend". Basically, it states that regardless of the answer on Test 2, if the partnership contains less than 80% (after the contribution), of its total assets of the following items, then the contributions to it do not require the recognition of gain. The items to be included in the 80% total are:

(This list was substantially changed in the Tax Reform Act of 1997 and is effective for transfers after June 8, 1997.)

1) Cash (the cash may be taken off this "tainted assets" list if it can be shown it is to be used to add to the value of non-tainted assets, such as real estate)
2) Stocks or other equity interest in corporations and evidences of indebtedness
3) Foreign currency
4) An interest in a REIT, common trust fund, mutual fund, publicly traded partnership, or other equity interest that are convertible or exchanged into the above.

5) Precious metals, (unless used in a business)
6) An interest in any entity whose assets substantially consist of the above items.

Of note, and interest to us, are the items not on the list:

1) Real Estate
2) Interests in Limited Liability companies or other partnerships, (except as they might be included in #6)
3) Life insurance contracts

And then of course there is one more step to take. If your transaction has flunked the tests up to this point, so that it might be taxed as an investment company and accordingly the gains and losses recognized on contribution, there is one more place to go for salvation. In some "newer" treasury regulation in which the treasury is trying to be "friendly" to these transactions, they approved the contribution by two or more people of already diversified portfolios into a partnership without causing it to be an investment company.

To be considered "already diversified" each of the portfolios to be contributed must be composed as follows and pass the following tests:

1) Not more than 25% of the value of its total assets are invested in the stock and securities of any one issuer, and
2) Not more than 50% of the value of its total assets are invested in the stock and securities of 5 or fewer issuers.

We hope this explanation is helpful and explains why we

commonly issue a legal opinion to non-diversification with each of our partnerships. And further, why, when large sums of new money or securities are to be contributed, your advisors need to be part of the team that examines the transaction.

Please consult you tax counsel before entering into any transaction which even hints at "diversification." These rules and the interpretations herein might change.

Appendix 2

A Checklist for Estate and Financial Planning

Introduction

This checklist covers only a small portion of the items to be considered in planning an estate or setting out your financial affairs. We have found it useful, you might as well.

A wise man once said, "You can tell the quality of a person's life by the questions they ask themselves." Perhaps the same is true about the quality of someone's financial and estate planner!

This list is arranged in several parts:
- General Information
- Trusts, Estates, Wills, etc.
- Family Limited Partnerships and Related Entities

Items that are General in Nature

1) Is client or spouse a U.S. citizen? If not, what is their nationality and residency status?

2) Does client or spouse plan any future changes in residency or citizenship?

3) Does client or spouse anticipate any future inheritances or gifts from others?

4) Does client or spouse have the ability to exercise or

influence any powers of appointment?

5) Does client or spouse act as trustee or co-trustee of any trusts?

6) Are the beneficiaries, contingent beneficiaries, owners, contingent owners, and annuitants, contingent annuitants of all life insurance, annuities, Totten Trusts and IRAs - 401(k) or pension accounts set up to client's maximum advantage?

7) Is either client or spouse divorced, or anticipating a divorce, either among themselves or their parents or children? Have they planned for that as a possibility? What are the details?

8) Does client or spouse have a prenuptial or postnuptial agreement?

9) Does client or spouse have children with special needs (financial, emotional, medical)?

10) Does client or spouse wish to disinherit any family member that perhaps has been otherwise provided for? OR Not otherwise provided for?

11) Has client or spouse ever promised or expressed an intention to provide money or support for another person or organization (other than a family member included in estate plan) either during or after client's life? Could anyone have misinterpreted any actions and believe such a promise existed?

12) Has client or spouse ever adopted anyone for the convenience of that person, such as citizenship?

13) Is the control of their assets important to client and spouse? How important?

14) Are client and spouse competent, experienced, and interested in managing the financial affairs of the estate?

15) Within the family of client and spouse, are income tax savings possible by sharing the taxable income on each other's tax returns?

16) Are all appropriate and available family members using their Annual Gift Exclusions?

17) Does client and/or spouse have a history of making or receiving gifts? Do they want that continued in the event of their incapacity? Do they have a desire to start and continue such a program in the future?

18) Does client or spouse own, run, or control any corporations? What types are they? Are they provided for?

19) What type and nature of liability does the occupation of the client and/or spouse attract to them or their family?

20) Has client and/or spouse ever been involved in a civil action? What is their opinion of the court system?

21) Has client or spouse shown any unique successful managerial or professional business expertise or experience?

22) What does client expect to gain, save or change from the Estate/Financial planning process?

23) Is any family member or dependant ill, or ever likely to need long term medical care?

24) What is the family history (for client and spouse) for:
a) Life expectancy
b) Cancer
c) Mental accuracy
d) Heart attacks
e) Competency

25) Is client and/or spouse currently taking minimum required distributions from and IRA or 401(k) or Qualified Plan? To start soon?

26) Are the client's other professional advisors up to the task of understanding and implementing the necessary changes and administering the results without missing a beat?

27) Is the client/spouse current on their Federal and State Tax Filings?

28) Is the business of the client/spouse good, or a subject of concern? Is a transaction pending?

29) Is the client's business of a type or nature, which lends itself to being passed down to future generations or will it likely be sold? Is it ready?

30) Is a succession plan in place with instructions as to how to best dispose of business assets or interest at the best prices? Successive managers and administrators named? Compensation for them determined?

31) If the business is to be sold or liquidated has a tax plan been considered?

32) Does client/spouse understand that there is no step-up in tax basis for:
   a) IRA's and 401(k)'s, and Pension Plans
   b) Savings Bonds
   c) Installment sales
   d) Annuities
   e) Net unrealized appreciation on Distributions of Employer Securities Form A QRP

33) Does client understand "double taxation" of Annuities, IRAs, 401(k)s, and Pension accounts?

34) Does client understand that life insurance "owned" by the decedent is included and may be taxed in their estate? Have solutions to this been proposed?

35) Have the financial needs of the extended family and friends of client and spouse been considered?
   a) Has long term health costs been considered for parents and elders?
   b) Has Medicaid planning been considered for parents and elders?
   c) Do all family members have appropriate health care coverage (i.e., students taking a year off may not be covered by parents' policies?
   d) Umbrella liability coverage for client/spouse and extended family and friends?

36) Are the assets of the client and spouse likely to continue to grow? What will they be like if client lives to normal life expectancy? To the normal life expectancy of the family memebers?

37) At the respective deaths of the client and spouse are their combined assets (including life insurance they own, inheritances and gifts they might receive in the meantime and growth on their money) likely to be

in excess of the Unified Credit amount currently
$625,000 each?

38) Is client or spouse a spender or a saver? Do this
issue need to be addressed in the plan?

39) Future plans of client as to work or retirement?

40) Does client or spouse have a unique or special voca-
tion or avocation which needs to be considered in
the plan?

41) Are client's objectives reasonable? Do they conflict
with those of the spouse? Does this difference, if
any, need to be considered in the plan?

42) Is the current financial estate plan of the client's
spouse set up to accomplish any of the following:
a) minimize income taxes?
b) minimize estate taxes?
c) reduce estate administration fees?
d) keep control in the hands of client and spouse
during their lives?
e) recognize the potential need for Medicaid?
f) protect assets transferred from being spent by the
recipients or seized by creditors?

43) Is client/spouse compounding their tax liability to
favor the government?

44) Will a valuation discount help reduce taxes for the
client/spouse?

45) Does client/spouse wish to leave "income only"
interest to certain people?

46) Does client see the positive and negative in leaving
outright bequests to beneficiaries?

Such as:
a) Income in the estate?
b) Subject to their creditors' claims?
c) Subject to being spent?
d) Subject to poor or inconstant investment strategies?
e) Subject (perhaps) to the Generation Skipping? Tax- or being included in many successive estates?
f) Subject to the " Best intentioned spouse rule"?

47) Is the client using up Generation Skipping Tax exemption by making gifts in trust? Is client/spouse not using GST annual exclusion?

48) Have appropriate parties been notified of the plan:
a) Accountant?
b) Real Estate Attorney?
c) Brokerage Firms and Mutual Fund?
d) Life Insurance companies?

49) Has client been advised of appropriate review period for estate plans? What type of events suggest a review:
a) Death of family member
b) Illness
c) Inheritance
d) Retirement
e) Sale of business
f) Change in income or financial circumstances
g) Divorce or re-marriage, of client or any family member
h) Change of residence
i) Change in laws or tax rates
j) Offers of retirement or purchase of business
k) Children moving out or back into home
l) Children, grandchildren, great-grandchildren being born or married

50) Is client/spouse concerned about gifting as it pertains to:
a) Loss of the funds?
b) Loss of control of the funds?
c) Loss of diversification of the investment portfolio?
d) Loss of income off the funds?
e) Loss of parental input/control?
f) Loss on the part of the child of their values?
g) Loss of motivations to work and produce?
h) Possible creditor or divorce claims from child or child's spouse?

51) Is safety deposit box appropriately located and access properly titled?

52) Is client aware of amenability provisions and of which type of documents can be changed in the future and which can't?

53) Does client or spouse own any highly appreciated securities? If yes, are they in need of more spendable income in exchange for no capital gains on the property? Are they willing to give up some of the future appreciation on the appreciated property in exchange for that income?

54) Is client/spouse either insurable for life insurance purposes?

55) Does client wish the method of investing for their trusts or funds to be prudent man, prudent investor or businessman? Do they desire standards to change for successive managers?

56) Are you aware of any documents of the Client/Spouse antiquated by law, or the passage of time, or other event?

57) Does the plan developed need to slowly or quickly, (or not at all), move control of business or investments from one generation to another?

58) Is client/spouse/parent a procrastinator, such that it might interfere with the savings the plan can generate?

59) Have any valuable family heirlooms or "stories" been preserved so that they may be passed down generationally?

60) Have elders spoken with the holders, to the health care surrogate, and/or living will to instruct them how they want decisions made?

61) Has senior family member divided up special property (heirlooms, furniture, jewelry, etc.) via special list and, if final, given copies of the list to all parties?

62) Have senior family members chosen an Advisor(s) to recommend to heirs and administrators to ease their headache? Have they been introduced? Has a pre-need agreement been executed?

63) Has elder chosen in advance of any incapacity or illness an adult congregate living facility or retirement home, as waiting for children to chose my be uneconomic and unduly stressful?

64) Does grandparent wish to spend more time with grandchildren vis-a-vis a business relationship to help them bond? What type of capacity?

65) Will the various documents prepared to assist the administration of the money or the estate be respect-

ed in the jurisdiction and by the institutions where they will be needed?

66) Has nursing home checklist been consulted if appropriate?

67) If multi-state residency is a possibility, has the time and care been taken to chose the best state for person's tax home and plan to make that election stick?

68) Has client been instructed to leave a list of important documents and their locations for future administrators?

69) If Medicaid planning is a possibility, has client been informed that state laws vary greatly in their collection of Medicaid liens? Also, importance of state of residency in such matters?

70) Does issue of another state taxing for income and estate taxes retirement benefits earned in that state but collected in a "tax-free" state exist?

71) Does client maintain their tax home in one state or county while spouse uses another?

72) In spite of existence of Living Will and health care surrogate, has elder discussed with strong willed family members the existence of those documents?

73) Will anticipated changes in residency, or financial status, or other items require changes in plan and if so should those changes in the plan be made after the change or before?

74) Does client/spouse understand the current risk/rewards on their investments?

75) Is persistent inflation and cost of living increase hurting the value of the income from the fixed income portfolio of the client/spouse?

76) Is client/spouse/responsible children or parents in debt to expensive financial institution and if yes, is there a solution via intrafamily loans?

77) Does client/spouse have enough net cash flow to function?

78) Does client use multiple financial advisors or brokers? Has consolidation been considered?

79) Is client/spouse currently ill? Have items such as disability insurance, home heath care, Medicare Gap insurance and long-term care been considered for issue or claim?

80) If client is sick, has claim been made for Waiver of Premium benefits disability claims, SSI claims etc?

81) If client is forgetful, did we check:
   a) Any liens against person?
   b) Check credit report?
   c) Check for payment of property taxes?
   d) Tax returns, federal filed and taxes paid?
   e) Tax returns, state filed and taxes paid?
   f) Addresses changed to be appropriate?
   g) Living trust funded, all assets possible?
   h) Checks of payments on direct deposit?
   i) Lease/contractual obligations current they must do?
   j) Any wasted assets to be recovered and put to work?
   k) Check driver's license record?
   l) Check under former married names or aliases as well?

m) Have monies due person actually been paid, rents, dividends, interest?

n) Think!

82) Has client verified employment FICA payments with Social Security system recently? Spouse? Others in family?

83) Is family concerned about "unhealthy" or "unexpected" alliances between elder and non-family members (i.e., nurses?). If so, has "family care agreement" been executed with appropriate consideration?

84) Are all trustees, personal representative general partners, etc. aware of their responsibility to file necessary tax reporting forms?

85) If any family member is ill or has a special condition, are they members of the appropriate support groups?

86) If any person is excluded from an inheritance, are they mentioned in the will as a zero?

87) If any provision in one will is dependant upon another, is that specified and/or contractual? For example, wife provides for Johnny so husband does. Husband dies first then wife changes mind. Johnny gets nothing despite dad's intent otherwise.

88) If elderly, does client/spouse have a case manager? Who? Are they informed?

89) Does client/spouse have difficulty facing these issues? What is strategy to overcome this reluctance?

90) In a death bed planning situation, has the following been considered:
   a) Selling off tax losses?
   b) Consolidating all securities to ease administration?
   c) Living will, health care surrogate, etc.?
   d) All family members aware of desires of elder, re: living will?
   e) Any lifetime elections made either under will or not, also disclaimers?
   f) Any depositions, interrogatories statements to understanding or interoperations to anything they were witness to, completed?
   g) Any strategies that might help family later on, last minute gifting payment of other medical costs or schooling?
   h) Payment of back Trustee fees to others?.
   i) "Beamed theory" FLP possible?
   j) Check beneficiaries on life annuity and IRA for appropriateness?
   k) Use of second to die life insurance?
   l) Sell, hard to sell, or hard to value items to ease administration?
   m) Secure home and valuables from loss?
   n) Consider resigning as trustee of living trust to ease payment of fees.
   o) Is elder in any multi-level marketing business that may be transferred during life, or insurance agent?
   p) Has a transfer of appreciated property to a spouse for basis setup been considered? (1 year wait)
   q) Death bed "Roth conversion?"

91) Does trustee of Living Trust get to make gifts, set up FLP, continue gift giving program, etc.?

92) Does plan provide for compensation to family members acting as caregivers?

93) Do pre-1977 spousal joint tenancy rules provide any benefit in income or estate tax planning?

94) Has a successor custodian been appointed for each transfer to minor's account? Trusts, Estates, Will and Probate

95) Does the governing document specify application of the income and principal rules or does it allow the trustee to make flat payments to benefit income beneficiaries?

96) If QDOT Trust is involved for a person who is not a U.S. citizen, are the assets likely to be over $2,000,000?

97) Who does client/spouse trust to be:
   a) Pre-need guardian for their person?
   b) Pre-need guardian for their assets?
   c) Durable Power of Attorney holder (and 3 successors)?
   d) Guardian for each child (and 3 successors)?
   e) Trustees of their money?
   f) To raise any minor children?
   g) Trustees of their children's, grandchildren's inheritances?
   h) Successor custodian under the Uniform Transfers to Minors Act?

98) Has client been advised of a possibility for a discount via an advance agreement letter with law firm?

99) If client is using an A/B Trust, are their assets set up

to allow funding of that trust and thereby utilize the unified credits? If not possible, have alternative been explained?

100) Has defective trust been considered? Reciprocal trust rules considered?

101) Has Generation Skipping Tax possibilities been considered?

102) Does Will/Trust contain pecuniary bequests?

103) Are Social Security taxes being properly handled?

104) Does plan provide for multi successor trustees?

105) Does a reverse mortgage exist, or is it being considered? Options on death?

106) Do all businesses that family has an interest in have:
   a) Succession plan in writing?
   b) Employee being trained to take over?
   c) Instruction to sell or liquidate, (who are you going to call?)
   d) Location of any secret documents or codes necessary to operate business produce product or key in equipment?

Family Limited Partnerships

107) Does client/spouse have the type and size of assets/desires to warrant a Family Limited Partnership?

108) Has client/spouse/accountant kept track of the cost basis of assets?

109) Is client paying unnecessary state income taxes or costs by an inefficient choice of state for FLP or business?

110) Has all real estate that was contributed been reviewed for liabilities and negative tax basis and recapture problems?

111) Have all costs of transfer doc stamps, etc. been considered in the transaction?

112) Does real property have any special tax exclusions, waivers, permits, land use restrictions, tax abatements, zoning requirements, etc., that may be affected by transfer or change in title?

113) Have business purpose and investment policy statements been prepared and approved by client?

114) Is this a Stealth Plan?

115) Has an annual budget for the operation of the FLP been explained to the client?

116) If client/spouse is a Limited Partner or shareholder in a closely held corporation or Limited Liability Company, is an appropriate buy-sell agreement in place with appropriate funding mediums and agreements with restrictions set up?

117) If FLP is set up, does it have a reasonable expectation of funds to pay for its operations and investments (like insurance premiums)?

118) Has appraisal been ordered for any discountable entity?

119) Has client been advised of the normal operating costs of FLP or Limited Liability Company?

120) Does FLP contain a non-attributable person in mix?

121) All annuities to be transferred to FLP issued, or deemed issued, after the appropriate date?

122) If life insurance is to be transferred to FLP, is insured one of the partners?

123) If life insurance to be owned or premiums paid by FLP, is FLP the beneficiary?

124) Is part of the plan for a partnership to redeem any partners' partnership interest?

125) Have standard loan documents been issued to document any loans (plus further advances) to any partner in accordance with Limited Partner agreement?

126) If non-Florida FLP with Florida General Partner, is statement switch page in effect?

127) Will client/spouse prepare annual notice of meeting, minutes, summary report or shall we?

128) Are any lottery winnings transferred into FLP done on a pre-tax or after-tax basis? At time of registration of the win or subsequent? By assignment or purchase and sale?

129) Is FLP to be used, in part, to qualify others for ROTH Ira? Describe methodology used?

130) Is FLP being used to protect the assets of, or the

assets to be given to, younger generations from waste?

131) If FLP owns, or will own, term insurance, how is premium to be treated?

132) If FLP party to Buy-Sell or Cross-Purchase agreement between different holders of a investment item, or business interest, or between LPs and General Partners for partnership interests is:

a) The agreement signed and formal?
b) Is the agreement funded or financing options otherwise agreed to?
c) Are all parties that will live with the agreement aware of the ramifications?
d) How will debts owed by the business interests or Limited Partner and guaranteed by the General Partner or Limited Partner be treated?

133) Is "beaming-transfer" theory being used in this case?

134) Any unusual financial circumstances, contractual agreements, or realities to be dealt with or acknowledged?

135) Does plan anticipate contribution of property into FLP, subject to formal or casual liabilities, or life estates, or payments? Approval or changes accepted by parties?

136) Is niece or nephew or other 2704(b) stranger a Limited Partner or General Partner with power to stop termination?

137) Does FLP trustee have authority in trust to act?

138) Has possibility of multi-level FLPs been considered? Combinations?

139) Is the FLP/Limited Liability Company under consideration to be amended or restated versions of a former one?

140) Fraudulent conveyance issues discussed?

141) Any special voting considerations via any special documents?

142) Any challenge from non-diversification rules?

143) Appropriate appraisals ordered and results used to base values on?

144) Any special type of property, which might aid in the valuation efforts being contributed? Considered?

145) Is a trust "c" Corp., or other FLP, a Limited Partner in this plan? Tax and cash flow aspects considered?

146) Are all brokers, agents advisors, consultants, where necessary, licensed in the state or Situs of FLP or other Entity?

Appendix 3

Listing of Professionals

Want help figuring out your estimated tax savings?

Order your FAMILY LIMITED PARTNERSHIP ESTIMATOR, VERSION 1.1 © **today!!!**

Order Your Disk Today!!! $19.95 plus $2.50 S&H (800) 950-9116

The professionals listed here have expressed an emphasis on the use and implementation of Family Limited Partnerships. We encourage you to seek their assistance in implementing your own Family Limited Partnership.

We realize all states are not represented. This index is continually updated. Please visit our site at www.stoll-fin.com on the World Wide Web for the updates or call Fortune Press Publishers at 1-800-950-9116.

ALABAMA
FINANCIAL ADVISOR

Stephen T. Satterlee, Senior Advisor
Gilsbar Advisory, Inc.
(Registered Investment Advisor)
2100 Covington Centre
Covington, LA 70433
Phone: **(504) 898-1572 or**
(800) 445-7227 Ext. 572
FAX: **(504) 898-1730**

Areas of Focus:
Specializes in Financial and Estate planning from a macroeconomic planning stand point showing clients how to create wealth while protecting their wealth from being transferred to financial institutions, corporations and the Federal Govenment.

Biography:
B.S. degree in Real Estate (finance) from Florida State University.
Began work experience on the financial side at IBM Corporation
Over eleven years of experience in the financial arena.
Experienced in the use and implementation of Family Partnerships in the planning process. Formed Stephen T. Satterlee, LLC
Member of the IAFP, ICFP, and Northshore Estate Planning Council.
Services also offered in Louisiana, Mississippi and the Florida Panhandle.

James Jay Morris
2105 Whiting Road
Hoover, AL 35216
Phone: (205) 822-1179
         (800)970-9713
FAX: (205)822-2279
         (800)970-9717

Areas of Focus:
Specializes in the use and implementation of Family Partnerships

FLORIDA
ATTORNEY

Alan S. Gassman
Gassman & Conetta, PA
1245 Court Street, Suite 102
Clearwater, Florida 34616
Phone: (727) 442-1200
FAX: (727) 443-5829

Areas of Focus:
Estate and Tax Planning, Physician Representation
Corporate Business Law
Biography:
Graduated Rollins College (B.A., with distinction, 1980),
University of Floida (J.D. with honors,1982, L.L.M. in Taxation
1983). The firm of Gassman & Conetta, PA was formed in 1986
by Alan S. Gassman who was formerly a partner in the
Clearwater Law Firm of Larson, Conklin,Stanley, Probst, and
Gassman. Tami Conetta joined the firm in 1990 and became a
partner in 1995.

Edwin B. Kagan
Edwin B. Kagan, P.A.
2709 Rocky Point Dr., Suite 102
Tampa, Florida   33607
Phone: (813)281-5609
FAX: (813)288-0428

Areas of Focus:
Securities and Corporate Law
Representation of individuals and closely-held businesses in the
areas of asset protection and business planning.
Biography:
Graduated University of Miami (J.D.,cum laude, 1976), Cornell
University (B.S.., 1973). Sole practice since 1988, was a partner
in various law firms (1983-1987), Attorney for the U.S. Securities
and Exchange Commision (1976-1982)

William K. Lovelace
Ford and Lovelace, P.A
2310 West Bay Drive
Largo, Florida 33770
Phone: (727) 581-9421
FAX: (727) 581-9422

Areas of Focus:
Emphasis on the use and implementation of Family Limited
Partnerships Will, Trusts, Probate, Irrevocable Trusts
Business and Corporate Planning
Biography:
Advanced degree (L.L.M.) in Taxation from University of
Florida, Juris Doctorate from Mississippi College of Law
Member of the Clearwater Bar Association, Pinellas County
Estate Planning Council, Bellair Florida Rotary, Network
Professionals

Bernard A. Singer, Esq.
Bernard A. Singer, P.A.
4925 Sheridan Street, Suite A
Hollywood, FL 33021
Broward: (954) 985-8600
Palm Bch: (561) 347-0577
Dade: (305) 892-8512
FAX: (954) 985-8477

Areas of Focus:
Family Partnerships, Life Insurance Trusts, Qualified Residence
Trusts, Revocable Trusts, Income and Estate Tax planning
Biography:
Certified by the Florida Bar as a Specialist in Tax law
J.D. Degree from University of Miami
B.S. Degree from Northeastern University
Worked as Certified Public Accountant with Ernst & Young and as
Tax Manager of Lennar Corporation
Since 1977 Mr. Singer has practiced as an attorney in South Florida
Member of AICPA, FICPA, Florida Bar, Greater Ft. Lauderdale Tax
Council

Ronald C. White, Esquire
Ronald C. White, P.A.
5348 First Avenue North
St. Petersburg, Florida 33710
Phone: (727) 323-5700
FAX: (727) 327-0930
E-Mail: rcw@gate.net

Areas of focus:
Emphasis on the use and implementation of Family Limited
Partnerships Practice includes Wills, Estates, and Business Planning
Biography:
Juris Doctorate degree from Baylor School of Law 1976, Private prac-
tice since 1981. Currently a Lt. Colonel in the United States Air
Force Reserve. Member of St. Petersburg Bar Association and com-
158 mittee member of the Trust Law Section of the Florida Bar.

ACCOUNTANTS

Randall W. Drew
Progressive Financial, Inc.
5533 Central Avenue, Suite B
St. Petersburg, Florida 33310
Phone: (727) 347-4909
FAX: (727) 381-8477

Areas of Focus:
New Ventures (Business and Real Estate)
Analyzing from a complete perspective
Incorporating business tax and financial dynamics into a
solid plan
Biography:
Began in own business in 1985 EA (enrolled to represent
clients before the IRS). Instructor for SBA seminars, estate
board, local college, and accounting associations. Member
of National Society of Public Accountants

FINANCIAL ADVISORS

Mary Lou James, President
8268 Berkeley Manor Blvd.
Financial Focus Group, Inc.
Spring Hill, FL 34606
Phone: (352) 597-5821
FAX: (352) 597-5827
Areas of Focus:
Long Term Care Specialist which includes a myriad of financial issues for
the elderly such as Miller Trusts, Medicare & Medicaid guidelines for
home health, assisted living facilities and nursing homes, extensive data-
base on facilities in Hernando County and utilization of techniques
including Family Limited Partnerships to determine the best way to pay
for these services.
Biography:
B.S. in Education Degree from Southern Connecticut State University,
Certified Financial Planner. Over 15 years experience in all areas of
insurance and financial planning including securities. Member various
local service groups and active in youth ministry.

Robert Herget
The Herget Company
9700 S. Dixie Highway, Suite 660
Miami, FL 33156
Phone: (305) 670-2158
FAX: (305) 670-2161

Areas of Focus:
Specializes in the use and implementation of Family
Limited Partnerships, Employee Benefits, Securities
        Biography:
Bachelor of Arts Principia College. Employed by The
Herget Company for 14 years-owner for the past 11 years.
Member of National Association of Life Underwriters and
board member of The University Club.

Hal Rogers, CFP, President
Retirement Services
8800 Arlington Expressway
Jacksonville, FL 32211
Phone: (904) 725-0556
FAX: (904) 720-1909

Areas of Focus:
Specializing in retirement and estate planning
        Biography:
B.A. degree from University of North Florida, Certified
Financial Planner, Registered Investment Advisor. Financial
Planning since August 1982, previous Prudential Bache
Securities, Retirement Services since Jan. 1986.

Joseph Jiovenetta
Jiovenetta and Associates, Inc.
2151 W. Hillsboro Blvd., Suite 206
Deerfield Beach, FL 33442
Phone: (954) 428-5008
FAX: (954) 428-5738

Areas of Focus:
Business Succesion Planning
Estate Planning and Investment Planning
Biography:
Bachelor of Arts degree from Simpson College,
Disablity Consultant for Paul Revere. Began Jiovenetta
and Associates in 1986. Member of Million Dollar
Round Table, NAHU, AMCLU, NALU

Michael Rogan
ADS Advisors
670 Second St. N.
Safety Harbor, FL 34695
Phone: (800) 843-2244
FAX: (727) 725-8911

Areas of Focus:
Specializing in complete financial, estate, insurance and
tax planning.
Biography:
Bachelor of Arts in Economics, University of Virginia,
1985. Licensed Securities Broker since 1986, Registered
Investment Advisor since 1994. Member of NASD,
U.S. Junior Chamber of Commerce (dJaycees) and
Seroma International.

Charles S. Stoll, President
Stoll Financial Corp.
980 North Federal Highway, Suite 307
Boca Raton, Florida   33432
Phone: (561) 367-9111 or
**   (800) 950-9112**
FAX: (561)367-7312 or
**   (800) 950-7312**
E-Mail: css@gate.net

Areas of Focus:
Specializes in the use and implementation of Family Limited
Partnerships, Asset Allocation, Wealth Creation and Preservation
        Biography:
B.A. degree from Stetson College, Certified Financial Planner,
Certified Public Accountant, Certified Estate Planner and
Personal Financial Specialist. Worked with Paine Webber and
Sherson Lehman, formed Stoll Financial Corp. in 1989.
Member of the AICPA.

C. Raymond Weldon
Weldon and Company
Registered Investment Advisor
1550 Madruga Avenue, Suite 318
Coral Gables, Florida 33146
Phone: (305) 663-7357
FAX: (305) 663-7355

Areas of Focus:
Specializes in the use and implementation of:
Family Limited Partnerships, Personal Financial Engineering,
Business, and Transfer Planning
        Biography:
Bachelor of Science degree in finace from the University of
Florida, C. Raymond Weldon & Associates Financial Planning
since 1980, Incorporated, 1993. Registered Representative
Phoenix Equity Planning Corp. since 1982.

FLORIDA PANHANDLE
FINANCIAL ADVISOR

Stephen T. Satterlee, Senior Advisor
Gilsbar Advisory, Inc.
(Registered Investment Advisor)
2100 Covington Centre
Covington, LA 70433
Phone: (504) 898-1572 or
**   (800) 445-7227 Ext. 572**
FAX: (504) 898-1730

Areas of Focus:
Specializes in Financial and Estate planning from a macro-economic planning stand point showing clients how to create wealth while protecting their wealth from being transferred to financial institutions, corporations and the Federal Govenment.

Biography:
B.S. degree in Real Estate (finance) from Florida State University.
Began work experience on the financial side at IBM Corporation
Over eleven years of experience in the financial arena.
Experienced in the use and implementation of Family Partnerships in the planning process. Formed Stephen T. Satterlee, LLC
Member of the IAFP, ICFP, and Northshore Estate Planning Council.
Services also offered in Louisiana, Mississippi and the Florida Panhandle.

Services also offered in Louisiana, Alabama and Mississippi.

GEORGIA

FINANCIAL ADVISOR

James D. Sadlier
The Advisors Group
900 Ashwood Parkway, Suite 100
Atlanta, GA 30338
Phone: (770) 396-6733
FAX: (770) 641-6273

Areas of Focus:
Specializes in the use and implementation of trusts and
Family Partnerships
Biography:
Bachelor of Arts degree from Brookly College, MBA New
York Universtiy, Floor Trader American Stock Exchange,
Merrill Lynch, The Advisor Group

164

LOUISIANA
FINANCIAL ADVISOR

**Stephen T. Satterlee, Senior
Advisor
Gilsbar Advisory, Inc.
(Registered Investment Advisor)
2100 Covington Centre
Covington, LA 70433
Phone: (504) 898-1572 or
           (800) 445-7227 Ext. 572
FAX: (504) 898-1730**

Areas of Focus:
Specializes in Financial and Estate planning from a macroeconomic planning stand point showing clients how to create wealth while protecting their wealth from being transferred to financial institutions, corporations and the Federal Govenment.

Biography:
B.S. degree in Real Estate (finance) from Florida State University.
Began work experience on the financial side at IBM Corporation
Over eleven years of experience in the financial arena.
Experienced in the use and implementation of Family Partnerships in the planning process. Formed Stephen T. Satterlee, LLC
Member of the IAFP, ICFP, and Northshore Estate Planning Council.
Services also offered in Louisiana, Mississippi and the Florida Panhandle.

Services also offered in Alabama, Mississippi and the Florida Panhandle.

MARYLAND
FINANCIAL ADVISORS

Marc S. Schliefer, CFP
Equity Planning Institute, Inc.
7910 Woodmont Avenue, Suite 540
Bethesda, Maryland 20814
Phone: **(301) 652-8792**
(800) WLTHMAX
FAX: **(301) 652-9066**

Areas of Focus:
Creating and preserving the maximum amount of wealth
for clients

Biography:
Business and Accounting degree from University of
Maryland, 1978, Certified Financial Planner, 1984.
Financial Planner and Vice President of Equity Planing
since 1974 Member of Institute of Certified Financial
Planners, International Association of Financial
Planners, National Assoc. of Life Underwriters, board
member for several small companies and volunteer for
Make a Wish Foundation

Brian Campbell, MBA, CPA-PFS, CFP, RFC
Capital Solutions and Company, Incorporated
11140 Rockville Pike, Suite 400
Rockville, MD 20852-3144
Phone: **(301)881-7161** **FAX:** **(301)881-4026**

Areas of Focus:
Optimizes family wealth preservation through income and estate
tax reduction inheritance protection and estate maximization.

Biography:
MBA in Finance and Accounting from the University of
Maryland. Certified Public Accountant/Personal Financial
Specialist, Certified Financial Planner, Registered Financial
Consultant, Registered Investment and Licensed Insurance
Advisor.

MICHIGAN

FINANCIAL ADVISOR

Kenneth L. Osiwala
Osiwala & Associates Strategic Investment Services
3221 W. Big Beaver, Suite 101
Troy, MI 48084
Phone: (810) 649-2566
FAX: (810) 649-5515

Areas of Focus:
Specializing in educating clients on wealth creation and preservation strategies by the use of a financial engineering process.

Biography:
Bachelor of Arts in accounting from Oral Roberts University, worked with Ernest and Young previous to joining Osiwala and Associates.

Fortune Press Publishers
also offers the professional:

- Seminar Presentation Package
- Audio Tapes
- Marketing Package
- Consultation Programs

Call us at 1-800-950-9116 for more information

MISSISSIPPI
FINANCIAL ADVISOR

Stephen T. Satterlee, Senior Advisor
Gilsbar Advisory, Inc.
(Registered Investment Advisor)
2100 Covington Centre
Covington, LA 70433
Phone: (504) 898-1572 or
**   (800) 445-7227 Ext. 572**
FAX: (504) 898-1730

Areas of Focus:
Specializes in Financial and Estate planning from a macroeconomic planning stand point showing clients how to create wealth while protecting their wealth from being transferred to financial institutions, corporations and the Federal Govenment.

Biography:
B.S. degree in Real Estate (finance) from Florida State University.
Began work experience on the financial side at IBM Corporation
Over eleven years of experience in the financial arena.
Experienced in the use and implementation of Family Partnerships in the planning process. Formed Stephen T. Satterlee, LLC
Member of the IAFP, ICFP, and Northshore Estate Planning Council.
Services also offered in Louisiana, Mississippi and the Florida Panhandle.

Services also offered in Alabama, Louisiana and the Florida Panhandle.

NEW JERSEY

FINANCIAL ADVISOR

Robert J. DiQuollo
95 Madison Avenue, Suite 400
Morristown, New Jersey 07960
Phone: (973) 984-8860
FAX: (973) 2920003

Areas of Focus:
Tax, accounting, and fee only financial planning for executives, entre-
preneurs, trusts and family partnerships.
Biography:
Bachelor of Arts and MBA from Steton Hall University, Certified
Public Accountant, 1976, Personal Financial Specialist, 1991 and
Certified Financial Planner, 1996. Worked with Price Waterhouse and
Growth Bank. Formed DiQuollo & Co. 1988.

John L. Smallwood, CFP
39 Avenue at the Common
Shrewbury, NJ   07702
Phone: (908) 542-1565
FAX: (908) 389-0488

Areas of Focus:
Specializes in implementing strategic financial strategies

NORTH CAROLINA

ATTORNEY

Andrew A. Strauss
Strauss and Jones, P.A.
Suite 700, BB & T Building
One West Pack Square
Asheville, North Carolina 28801
Phone: (828) 258-0994
FAX: (828) 252-4921

Areas of Focus:
Family Partnerships, Estate Planning, Trusts and Estate Administration

FINANCIAL ADVISOR

Douglas D. Alden
Asheville Dollars & Sense
802 Fairview Road, Suite 300
Asheville, NC 28813-5459
Phone: (828) 299-7530
**   (800) 755-0466**
FAX: (828) 299-4341
E-Mail:ddalden@cheta.net

Areas of Focus:
Building, Enhancing, and Preserving Wealth from one generation to the next.
Biography:
Bachelor of Science degree from Western Michigan University, Chartered Life Underwriter (CLU), American College, Byrn Marr, PA. Twenty plus years experience in financial services in Florida and North Carolina. Member and officer of Harvest EPC, Asheville, North Carolina.

OHIO

Richard E. Villers
PRISM Financial
260 Northland Blvd., Suite 229
Cincinnati, OH 45246
Phone: **(513) 771-3332 or**
(800) 443-7526
FAX: **(513) 771-3352**
E-Mail: rvillerse@fuse.net

Areas of Focus:
Specializing in Estate Planning and Settlement
Utilizing Family Limited Partnerships
Biography:
Degree from the University of Akron. Attended the Phil
Heckering Institute of Estate Planning and the Loving
Trust Educational System. Formerly with Home
Federal Savings Bank, formed PRISM Financial in
1991.

OREGON

FINANCIAL ADVISOR

Barbara M. Seaman, LU TCS, RIC
Jeffrey J. Rickman
Genesis Financial Group, Inc.
2955 North Highway 97, Suite B
Bend, OR   97701
Phone: (541) 385-0798
FAX: (541) 382-3381

Areas of Focus:
Specializes in the use and implementation of Family Partnerships, charitable gifts, personal and corporate planning
Barbara's Biography:
Graduate of Syracuse University, New York with a Bachelor of Science in retail and management she has continued her education in Macro Economics and earned her Life Underwriters Training Counsel Fellowship (LUTCF). Has been advising individuals and business owners on their financial plans since 1986. She is a member of the Million Dollar Round Table.
Jeffrey's Biography:
Attended Carroll College, Helena, Montana. Worked as a Commercial Casually Underwriter and established Charitable/Estate Planning practice. Member of Chamber of Commerce, Bend Estate Planning Group. Awarded Perennial - President's Club Qualifier and Top Club Producer

PENNSYLVANIA

ATTORNEY

Peter J. Gilbert
Drake, Hileman, and Davis
Suite 15, Bailiwick Office Campus
P.O. Box 1306
Doylestown, PA   18901
Phone: (215) 348-2088
FAX: (215) 348-7069

Areas of Focus:
Concentrates on estate planning, including business succession
and Family Limited Partnerships
Biography
Bachelor of Arts degree from Haverford College, B.D. from Yale
Divinity School, Juris Doctorate Marshall-Wythe School of Law
(William & Mary) Employed by Drake, Hileman, & Davis since
1989. Member of Trust Counselor Network, Family Firm
Institue, Attorneys for Family Held Enterprises

FINANCIAL ADVISOR

Karen Ford
163 Woodhill Road
Newtown, PA 18940
Phone: (215) 860-6116
FAX: (215) 860-6404

Areas of Focus:
Specializes in creating wealth while reducing taxes

Gary P. Lux
Fortune Strategies
172 Churchville Lane
Churchville, PA 18966
Phone: (800) 871-5353
FAX: (215) 396-9183

Areas of Focus:
Financial and Estate planning for owners of closely held businesses.
Biography:
BBA in Accounting and Economic & Temple University 1978, Chartered Life Underwriters - American College 1983. New York Life Insurance Company since 1978. Founded Fortune Strategies 1987.

Neil J. Werberig
Maximum Asset Strategies
163 Woodhill Road
Newtown, PA 18940
Phone: (215)968-6088
FAX: (215)860-6404

Areas of Focus:
Investment Advisor specializing in maximum wealth creation through tax reduction and creative investment planning.
Biography:
Bachelor of Science degree from Pennsylvania State University in Aerospace Engineering. New York Life since 1973, NYLIFE Securites since 1984, formed Maximum Asset Strategies as a Registered Investment Advisor in 1987. Member of the Million Dollor Round Table and National Association of Life Underwriters

UTAH

FINANCIAL ADVISOR

George E. Moldenhauer
Black Diamond Asset Management
312 S. Main St., Box 719
Park City, UT   84060
Phone: (801)647-0709
FAX: (801) 647-9478

Areas of Focus:
Dynamic investment strategies and the use of Family Partnerships Free Initial
Consultation

CATCH US ON THE WEB

For an update on recent professionals visit us
on the web at http://www.stoll-fin.com or
contact us by phone 800-950-9116,
fax 800-950-7312 or mail.
Our address: Fortune Press Publishers, Inc.
980 North Federal Highway, Suite 307
Boca Raton, Florida 33432

VIRGINIA

FINANCIAL ADVISOR

Equity Concepts, Inc.
4510 Cox Road, Suite 303
Glen Allen, VA 23060
Phone: (804) 527-1863
FAX: (804) 527-3990

Areas of Focus:
Financial Engineering firm devoted to using strategies
that are on the forefront of financial technology by
applying Family Partnerships and other key strategies
we assure that your family's wealth is properly protected and fully maximized.
Biography:
Micheal J. Thaler, President
B.S. degrees in Finance and Business Administration
from Old Dominion University. Owned and operated a
franchise for a major restaurant operation for ten years
before forming Equity Concepts, Inc. in 1991.

John B. Robinson, Vice President
B.S. degrees in Accounting and Business
Administration from the University of Delaware.
Worked in a broad range of financial areas before join-
ing Equity Concepts, Inc. in 1994.

WASHINGTON, D.C.
Three Miles from D.C.

FINANCIAL ADVISOR

Marc S. Schliefer, CFP
Equity Planning Institute, Inc.
7910 Woodmont Avenue, Suite 540
Bethesda, Maryland   20814
Phone: (301) 652-8792
**   800) WLTHMAX**
FAX: (301) 652-9066

Areas of Focus:
Creating and preserving the maximum amount of
wealth for clients
Biography:
Business and Accounting degree from University of
Maryland, 1978, Certified Financial Planner, 1984.
Financial Planner and Vice President of Equity Planing
since 1974 Member of Institute of Certified Financial
Planners, International Association of Financial
Planners, National Assoc. of Life Underwriters, board
member for several small companies and volunteer for
Make a Wish Foundation

Yes, I would like to be kept up to date on Family Limited Partnerships and their many uses:

I am, ☐ a professional and would like information about being in the index of the next printing of this book and on the world wide web page (www.stoll-fin.com)

☐ someone who has a Family Limited Partnership

☐ someone who is considering a Family Limited Partnership. (Mention in comments if you would like to be contacted)

My information:

Name: _____

Address:_____

City, State, Zip_____

Fax: _____

Phone: _____

E-mail _____ @ _____

Comments: _____

(If you want to stay informed but don't wish to disclose your name have your family lawyer send in the form in their name)

Please fax form to 800-950-7312 or E-mail information to css@gate.net or mail to:

Fortune Press Publishers, Inc.
129 NW 13th Street, Suite D-26
Boca Raton, FL 33432
1-800-950-9116

Want help figuring out your estimated tax savings?

FAMILY LIMITED
PARTNERSHIP
ESTIMATOR
VERSION 1.1©
$19.95

Order Your Disk Today!!!
$19.95 plus $2.50 S&H
(800) 950-9116

Library of Congress Catalog Card Number: 98-074585

ISBN: 0-9654605-1-7

Fortune Press Publishers, Inc.
129 NW 13th Street, Suite D-26
Boca Raton, FL 33432
1-800-950-9116